# ROUTLEDGE LIBRARY EDITIONS: GERMAN LITERATURE

Volume 20

# LUDWIG TIECK

# LUDWIG TIECK
## An Annotated Guide to Research

DWIGHT A. KLETT

LONDON AND NEW YORK

First published in 1993 by Garland Publishing Inc.

This edition first published in 2020
by Routledge
2 Park Square, Milton Park, Abingdon, Oxon OX14 4RN

and by Routledge
52 Vanderbilt Avenue, New York, NY 10017

*Routledge is an imprint of the Taylor & Francis Group, an informa business*

© 1993 Dwight A. Klett

All rights reserved. No part of this book may be reprinted or reproduced or utilised in any form or by any electronic, mechanical, or other means, now known or hereafter invented, including photocopying and recording, or in any information storage or retrieval system, without permission in writing from the publishers.

*Trademark notice*: Product or corporate names may be trademarks or registered trademarks, and are used only for identification and explanation without intent to infringe.

*British Library Cataloguing in Publication Data*
A catalogue record for this book is available from the British Library

ISBN: 978-0-367-41588-4 (Set)
ISBN: 978-1-00-301460-7 (Set) (ebk)
ISBN: 978-0-367-85608-3 (Volume 20) (hbk)
ISBN: 978-0-367-85615-1 (Volume 20) (pbk)
ISBN: 978-1-00-301390-7 (Volume 20) (ebk)

**Publisher's Note**
The publisher has gone to great lengths to ensure the quality of this reprint but points out that some imperfections in the original copies may be apparent.

**Disclaimer**
The publisher has made every effort to trace copyright holders and would welcome correspondence from those they have been unable to trace.

# LUDWIG TIECK
*An Annotated Guide to Research*

Dwight A. Klett

GARLAND PUBLISHING, INC. • NEW YORK & LONDON
1993

© 1993 Dwight A. Klett
All rights reserved

Library of Congress Cataloging-in-Publication Data

Klett, Dwight A.
    Ludwig Tieck : an annotated guide to research / by Dwight A. Klett.
      p.   cm. — (Garland reference library of the humanities ; vol. 902)
    Includes index.
    ISBN 0-8240-5622-1 (alk. paper)
    1. Tieck, Ludwig, 1773-1853—Bibliography.   I. Title. II. Series.
Z8879.63.K55   1993
[PT2540]
016.838'609—dc20
                                                                                   93-624
                                                                                        CIP

Printed on acid-free, 250-year-life paper
Manufactured in the United States of America

# Contents

*Introduction*   xiii

*List of Abbreviations*   xvii

  I. Bibliographies and Research Reports   3
    1. Bibliographies   3
    2. Research Reports   4

 II. Biography   7
    1. Comprehensive Overviews   7
    2. Specific Aspects of Tieck's Life   11
      a. Childhood, Years of Study and Travel (1773-1819)   11
      b. Years in Dresden, "Vorleseabende" (1819-1841)   13
      c. Years in Berlin, Death, and Funeral (1841-1853)   16
      d. Tieck's Library and Literary Remains   17
      e. Relations with Individuals   18
        *i*. American and British (Bannatyne, Coleridge, W. Irving, H.C. Robinson, Ticknor)   18
        *ii*. Austrian and German (Eichendorff, Freytag, Grillparzer, Mörike, Raumer, the Schlegels, Dorothea Tieck, Rahel Varnhagen)   20
        *iii*. Danish (Oehlenschläger)   21
        *iv*. French and Russian   22
    3. Miscellaneous   22

| | |
|---|---|
| III. Criticism: General | 25 |
|   1. General Introductions to Tieck's Oeuvre | 25 |
|   2. Tieck as Romantic Author | 27 |
|   3. Sources for Tieck's Works | 31 |
|     a. German | 31 |
|     b. Other | 32 |
|   4. Tieck's Works: Stylistic Analyses | 33 |
|   5. Tieck's Works: Thematic Studies | 34 |
|     a. Alienation | 34 |
|     b. Color, Synaesthetic Imagery | 34 |
|     c. The Demonic, Fateful, Supernatural | 36 |
|     d. Humor, Satire | 37 |
|     e. Incest | 38 |
|     f. Irony | 39 |
|     g. Landscape, Nature | 39 |
|     h. Society, Social Issues, Artist vs. Society | 40 |
|     i. Other | 42 |
|   6. Miscellaneous | 42 |
| IV. Criticism: Poetry | 43 |
|   1. General | 43 |
|   2. Poems from the *Gedichte* Collection (1821-1823) | 45 |
|   3. Other Poems | 47 |
| V. Criticism: Drama | 49 |
|   1. General | 49 |
|   2. Early Dramas | 50 |
|     a. General | 50 |
|     b. *Das Reh* (1790, pub. 1855) | 51 |
|     c. *Alla-Moddin* (1790-1791, pub. 1798) | 51 |
|     d. *Der Abschied* (1792, pub. 1798) | 52 |
|     e. *Karl von Berneck* (1793-1795, pub. 1797) | 52 |
|   3. Satirical Dramas | 52 |
|     a. General | 52 |
|       *i*. Sources | 52 |
|       *ii*. Satirical Dramas and Irony | 53 |
|       *iii*. Other | 54 |
|     b. *Der gestiefelte Kater* (1797) | 56 |
|     c. *Ritter Blaubart* (1797) | 58 |
|     d. *Prinz Zerbino* (1796-1798, pub. 1799) | 58 |

  e. *Die verkehrte Welt* (1798, pub. 1799)    58
 4. Dramas Based on Chapbooks    59
  a. General    59
   *i.* English and German Sources    59
   *ii.* Spanish Sources    60
   *iii.* Other    61
  b. *Leben und Tod der heiligen Genoveva* (1800)    62
  c. *Kaiser Octavianus* (1804)    63
  d. *Fortunat* (1816)    63

VI. Criticism: Prose Fiction    65
 1. General    65
 2. Contributions to Nicolai's *Straußfedern* (1795-1798)    70
 3. Tales Based on Chapbooks    72
  a. General    72
  b. "Die schöne Magelone" (1797)    72
  c. "Geschichtschronik der Schildbürger" (1797)    73
 4. Fairy Tale Novellas    73
  a. General    73
  b. "Der blonde Eckbert" (1797)    79
  c. "Der getreue Eckart und der Tannenhäuser" (1799)    86
  d. "Der Runenberg" (1804)    87
  e. "Liebeszauber" (1812)    90
  f. "Die Elfen" (1812)    90
 5. Later Novellas    91
  a. General    91
   *i.* Later Novellas and Young Germany    91
   *ii.* Other    92
  b. "Die Gemälde" (1822)    97
  c. "Der Geheimnisvolle" (1823)    97
  d. "Die Reisenden" (1824)    97
  e. "Musikalische Leiden und Freuden" (1824)    97
  f. "Dichterleben" (1826-1831)    98
  g. "Der funfzehnte November" (1827)    98
  h. "Der Alte vom Berge" (1828)    99
  i. "Der Mondsüchtige" (1832)    99
  j. "Eine Sommerreise" (1834)    99
  k. "Tod des Dichters" (1834)    100

        l. "Der Wassermensch" (1835)       100
        m. "Eigensinn und Laune" (1836)       100
        n. "Der junge Tischlermeister" (1836)       101
        o. "Des Lebens Überfluß" (1839)       101
    6. Novels       104
        a. General       104
            *i.* Sources       104
            *ii.* Other       104
        b. *William Lovell* (1793-1796, pub. 1795-1796)       105
        c. *Peter Lebrecht* (1795-1796)       111
        d. *Franz Sternbalds Wanderungen* (1798)       112
        e. *Der Aufruhr in den Cevennen* (1826)       116
        f. *Vittoria Accorombona* (1840)       117

VII. Criticism: Letters       121
    1. General       121
    2. Collections Encompassing Numerous Correspondents       122
    3. Letters to/from Individual Correspondents       124
        a. Friedrich and Sophie Tieck       124
        b. Goethe       125
        c. Jean Paul       125
        d. Romantic Generation       126
            *i.* The Schlegels (August Wilhelm, Dorothea, Friedrich)       126
            *ii.* Wackenroder       127
            *iii.* Others (Arnim, Görres, Jakob Grimm, E.T.A. Hoffmann, Kerner, Runge, Uhland)       128
        e. Dresden Circle       129
            *i.* Böttiger       129
            *ii.* Carus       130
            *iii.* Others (Bülow, Prinz Johann von Sachsen, Laun, Ida von Lüttichau, Uechtritz)       130
        f. Raumer       131
        g. Actors       132
            *i.* Devrient       132
            *ii.* Iffland       132
        h. Philosophers       133
            *i.* Fichte       133
            *ii.* Solger       133

i. Publishers 133
    *i.* Brockhaus 133
    *ii.* Zimmer 134
    *iii.* Others (Cotta, Frommann, Göschen, Max, Reimer, Voß & Leo) 134
j. Correspondents Associated with Tieck's Editorial Projects 136
    *i.* Anton von Hardenberg 136
    *ii.* Hartmann 136
    *iii.* Schlosser 136
k. Foreign Correspondents 137
    *i.* Coleridge 137
    *ii.* Ticknor 137
    *iii.* Austrians (Bayer, Castelli, Matthäus von Collin, Deinhardstein, Karoline von Pichler, Schreyvogel) 137
l. Others 138
    *i.* Known Correspondents (Bernhardi, Brinkman, Burgsdorff, Fritze, Grabbe, Gries, Hebbel, F.H. Jacobi, Klingemann, Köpke, Küstner, Menzel, Reuss, Riemer, Robert, Johanna Schopenhauer, Varnhagen von Ense, Wendt) 138
    *ii.* Unknown Correspondents 142

VIII. Tieck as Critic 143
  1. General 143
  2. Drama Criticism, Stage Reforms, Work as "Dramaturg" 144
    a. General 144
    b. Concerning Shakespeare, Jonson, the Elizabethan Drama 146
    c. Other 149
  3. Miscellaneous 150

IX. Tieck as Editor and Translator 151
  1. Editorial Work 151
    a. Medieval German Literature 151
    b. German Renaissance and Baroque Literature 153

      c. Schnabel's *Insel Felsenburg*, Lenz and Kleist
         Editions      154
      d. Other      155
   2. Translations      155
      a. From the English      155
         *i.* General      155
         *ii.* Shakespeare      156
         *iii.* Sheridan      158
         *iv.* Other      158
      b. From Middle High German      158
      c. From the Spanish      159
         *i.* Cervantes      159
         *ii.* Espinel      159

X. Tieck and Art, Music, Education, Philosophy, Politics, and Religion      161
   1. Art      161
      a. General      161
      b. Tieck and Runge      162
      c. Tieck, Wackenroder, and their Collaborative Projects *Herzensergießungen eines Kunstliebenden Klosterbruders* (1797) and *Phantasien über die Kunst* (1799)      164
      d. Other      165
   2. Music      167
   3. Education      169
   4. Philosophy      169
   5. Politics      170
   6. Religion      171

XI. Reception, Influence, Comparative Studies      173
   1. America      173
      a. General      173
      b. Hawthorne      174
      c. Loomis      175
      d. Poe      175
   2. Britain      176
      a. General      176
      b. Coleridge      177
      c. Shakespeare      177

|  |  |
|---|---|
| d. Webster | 177 |
| e. Wilde | 178 |
| 3. France | 178 |
|    a. General | 178 |
|    b. Flaubert | 179 |
|    c. Zola | 179 |
| 4. Germany | 180 |
|    a. General | 180 |
|    b. Goethe | 182 |
|    c. Schiller | 182 |
|    d. Wieland | 183 |
|    e. Romantic Generation | 183 |
|       i. Brentano | 183 |
|       ii. Eichendorff | 184 |
|       iii. Novalis | 185 |
|       iv. Others (Arnim, E.T.A. Hoffmann, Schumann) | 185 |
|    f. Young Germany | 186 |
|       i. Heine | 186 |
|       ii. Others (Gutzkow, Laube) | 186 |
|    g. Realists | 187 |
|       i. Hebbel | 187 |
|       ii. Immermann | 187 |
|       iii. Others (Grabbe, Ludwig, Mörike, Raabe) | 188 |
|    h. Others | 189 |
|       i. Eighteenth and Nineteenth Century (Carus, Jean Paul, Maler Müller) | 189 |
|       ii. Twentieth Century (Kafka) | 189 |
| 5. Italy | 190 |
| 6. Russia | 190 |
| 7. Sweden | 191 |
| *Index of Authors and Editors* | 193 |

# Introduction

Ludwig Tieck's enduring fame seems to be rooted most strongly in his international appeal. While he is certainly lauded in Germany for his leadership position within the Romantic Movement, his significant contributions to the national literary canon (especially in terms of the novella and the comedy), and his lifelong efforts concerning the reappraisal of early German literature, it is only outside of Germany where he appears to really come into his own. This is not surprising considering his keen, almost legendary interest in foreign languages and literatures, which manifests itself not only in his unparalleled achievements as translator, editor, philologist, and critic vis-à-vis such international luminaries as Shakespeare, Jonson, Cervantes, Calderón, and Dante, but also in his popularization of numerous foreign authors in Germany and, just as importantly, in the vast network of contacts he maintained during his lifetime to a plethora of distinguished writers and scholars throughout Europe and even in the New World.

Indeed, Tieck contributed so significantly to the intellectual life of countries outside of Germany that his name still possesses high recognition value in a wide variety of international contexts. Mention Shakespeare and the Elizabethan Drama, and we are bound to be reminded of Tieck's groundbreaking philological work on this subject as well as of the renowned "Schlegel-Tieck" Shakespeare translations. And one could certainly expect similar results from a mention of Cervantes and the Spanish theater, just as a discussion on the supernatural tales of Poe and Hawthorne may easily be punctuated by commentary surrounding Tieck's impact, especially in the areas of themes and style. Similarly, one can hardly speak of the role of Italy in German literature without paying homage to Tieck's *Reisegedichte* or his contributions to *Herzensergießungen eines kunstliebenden Klosterbruders*, nor is it possible to address oneself to the origins of the romantic movements of Denmark, Russia, and Sweden without reference to Tieck's influence on Oehlenschläger, Gogol, and Atterbom respectively. And the list goes on.

For further evidence of Tieck's importance abroad, we need only consider the fact that at least as much secondary literature surrounding his life and works has been generated outside of his native Germany as within – and, in addition, that the foreign materials tend, by and large, to be much more appreciative of their subject than their German counterparts. There may in fact be some truth to Segebrecht's contention (see no. 88) that the first important steps towards the rehabilitation of Tieck's image were taken on foreign soil (primarily in France and the United States) after his fortunes had declined perilously in Germany during the late nineteenth and early twentieth centuries, not in the least, it should be added, because of his failure to jump on the nationalistic bandwagon.

In light of the foregoing, it would seem natural that the present bibliography of the secondary literature on Tieck – the first of its kind ever published – should focus on his life and works particularly from the international perspective. To facilitate this, I have opted for a detailed table of contents (with corresponding text divisions) instead of a subject index to render the information surrounding Tieck accessible. It is thereby possible, on the one hand, to effectively highlight Tieck's achievements in their various national contexts – his work as translator in Chapter IX, for example, is organized according to language – and to encourage "browsing" through the text's different sections on the other. Only in this manner can especially those individuals active in fields other than *Germanistik* get an accurate feel not only for Tieck's true versatility and range, but also for what he could contribute to their specific research needs and interests. Seasoned Tieck scholars will, by contrast, certainly appreciate that materials pertaining to his individual works and life segments are logically grouped together, allowing the reader to make immediate comparisons between separate entries without having to thumb through the entire volume seeking scattered information.

Of course, should information relevant to a particular section be included elsewhere, all necessary cross references will be provided. As the reader will doubtless find, however, the total number of cross references is far from daunting. We may attribute this to the circumstance that the materials on Tieck seem to define their own categories in a rather organic manner, ruling out any sort of arbitrariness on the bibliographer's part. Where the bibliographer's presence is more acutely felt, though, is in the area of annotations. While these are designed to provide useful information on an item's focus, special contributions to research, and relative merit, they can never be free of a certain amount of subjectivity, and should be treated accordingly.

In creating a work such as this, it is tremendously difficult to make judgement calls as to which materials to include or omit – a task in no way simplified by the vast amount of material available on Tieck, and that in a surprising number of different languages. At any rate, the decision to limit the present bibliography to secondary sources was made early on in the conceptualization process, since Tieck's works have been recently and most painstakingly catalogued by Paulin (see no. 2), who lists all published works by Tieck (including background on first and subsequent editions), unpublished manuscripts (including locations), and works Tieck coauthored, translated, edited, and supplied with introductions. Translations of Tieck's works, incidentally, have also been omitted, as they are listed for the most part in nos. 660 (English), 676 (French), and 102 and 723 (Italian). Each of these items contains useful judgements concerning the relative quality of the translations cited.

The one exception I do make with reference to primary materials concerns Tieck's correspondence, which I include in Chapter VII under the heading "Criticism: Letters" because it has never before been assembled in one place, not even in the aforementioned work by Paulin. Most of the entries under this heading represent unpublished letters accompanied by extensive editorial and historical commentary, hence their inclusion under "criticism."

Turning again to the secondary sources around which this book revolves, I have – with very few exceptions – not included any treatments of Tieck's life and works as found in 1) literary histories and reference volumes, as these are widely available and, by definition, are often rather general in orientation; 2) popular magazines and contemporary memoirs, which typically lack critical depth; and 3) newspapers, reviews, obscure journals, and unpublished dissertations, because of their frequent inaccessibility. Where exceptions are made, especially in the case of unpublished dissertations, the reader is assured that they usually represent either unique or extremely interesting contributions to scholarship. Finally, I made it a point – again with a few notable exceptions – to exclude materials I have not actually had the opportunity to examine.

While this bibliography strives – intentional omissions aside – to be as comprehensive as possible (particularly also in terms of foreign-language items), it is bound to manifest occasional lacunae, especially considering the lack not only of a solid bibliographical base on Tieck, but also of any sort of international "Tieck Yearbook" or "Tieck Society," which could have aided my efforts. But, like most bibliographers, I did not have to go it entirely alone. Indeed, I am greatly indebted to Mary George, Head of the General and Humanities Reference Division in the Firestone Library of Princeton University, for her expertise in hunting down the most difficult-to-obtain items as well as for her advice vis-à-vis the creation of the ordering principle underlying the entire work. My gratitude also extends to the staff of the Interlibrary Loan Department in the Alexander Library of Rutgers University for cheerfully processing my seemingly endless stream of requests, to the Rutgers Faculty of Arts and Sciences for generously awarding me a Henry Rutgers Fellowship to conduct research at libraries throughout the United States and Germany, to the staffs of those libraries, who assisted me in uncountable ways, and to my wife Ulrike, whose professional advice and encouragement ultimately made this project possible.

New Brunswick, New Jersey<br>
November 1992

# List of Abbreviations

| | |
|---|---|
| *ActaG* | *Acta Germanica: Jahrbuch des südafrikanischen Germanistenverbandes* |
| *Anglia* | *Anglia: Zeitschrift für englische Philologie* |
| *Archiv* | *Archiv für das Studium der neueren Sprachen und Literaturen* |
| *AUMLA* | *Journal of the Australasian Universities Language and Literature Association* |
| *Aurora* | *Aurora: Jahrbuch der Eichendorff-Gesellschaft* |
| *CGP* | *Carleton Germanic Papers* |
| *CLS* | *Comparative Literature Studies* |
| *CollG* | *Colloquia Germanica* |
| *DAI* | *Dissertation Abstracts International* |
| *DU* | *Der Deutschunterricht* |
| *DVLG* | *Deutsche Vierteljahrsschrift für Literaturwissenschaft und Geistesgeschichte* |
| *EG* | *Etudes Germaniques* |
| *Euphorion* | *Euphorion: Zeitschrift für Literaturgeschichte* |
| *GL&L* | *German Life and Letters* |
| *GN* | *Germanic Notes* |
| *GQ* | *German Quarterly* |
| *GR* | *Germanic Review* |
| *GRM* | *Germanisch-romanische Monatsschrift* |

| | |
|---|---|
| IAN | Izvestiia Akademii Nauk S.S.S.R., Seriia Literatury i Iazyka |
| IASL | Internationales Archiv für Sozialgeschichte der deutschen Literatur |
| JDSG | Jahrbuch der deutschen Schiller-Gesellschaft |
| JDSh | Jahrbuch der deutschen Shakespeare-Gesellschaft |
| JEGP | Journal of English and Germanic Philology |
| JFDH | Jahrbuch des Freien Deutschen Hochstifts |
| JIG | Jahrbuch für internationale Germanistik |
| JJPG | Jahrbuch der Jean-Paul-Gesellschaft |
| JWGV | Jahrbuch des Wiener Goethe-Vereins |
| LJGG | Literaturwissenschaftliches Jahrbuch im Auftrage der Görres-Gesellschaft |
| MAL | Modern Austrian Literature |
| MGS | Michigan Germanic Studies |
| MLN | Modern Language Notes |
| MLQ | Modern Language Quarterly |
| MLR | Modern Language Review |
| Monatshefte | Monatshefte für deutschen Unterricht, deutsche Sprache und Literatur |
| NG | Neue Germanistik |
| NGS | New German Studies |
| OGS | Oxford German Studies |
| PEGS | Publications of the English Goethe Society |
| PMLA | Publications of the Modern Language Association of America |
| PQ | Philological Quarterly |
| RGer | Recherches Germaniques |
| RLC | Revue de Littérature comparée |
| Selecta | Selecta: Journal of the Pacific Northwest Council on Foreign Languages [Formerly Proceedings: Pacific Northwest Conference on Foreign Languages] |
| Seminar | Seminar: A Journal of Germanic Studies |
| SIR | Studies in Romanticism |
| UP | Die Unterrichtspraxis |
| VMU | Vestnik Moskovskogo Universiteta, Seriia 9: Filologiia |

| | |
|---|---|
| WB | *Weimarer Beiträge* |
| WW | *Wirkendes Wort* |
| ZDP | *Zeitschrift für deutsche Philologie* |

# Ludwig Tieck

# I. Bibliographies and Research Reports

## 1. BIBLIOGRAPHIES

1. Falkenberg, Hans-Geert. "Strukturen des Nihilismus im Frühwerk Ludwig Tiecks." Diss. Göttingen, 1956.

   Appended to this study of nihilistic elements in *William Lovell* and other early works (see also no. 234) is an extensive general Tieck bibliography for the years 1835-1962. Although it represents a valiant attempt at filling a blatant gap in Tieck scholarship, this chronologically organized bibliography makes a poor reference tool not only because it is largely inaccessible and is fraught with serious errors and omissions (coverage for 1956-1962, added later, is especially shaky), but also because it lacks customary headings and divisions as well as consistent annotations and cross references.

2. Paulin, Roger. *Ludwig Tieck*. Sammlung Metzler, Vol. 185. Stuttgart: J.B. Metzler, 1987. vi + 133 pp.

   A useful reference volume containing Tieck's complete primary bibliography, that is, his independent literary and critical works as well as works he coauthored, translated, edited, and supplied with introductions (with all data on first publication and subsequent inclusion in various editions noted). Also lists Tieck's unpublished writings, citing the location of all manuscripts. However, contains only a modest selection from the vast body of secondary literature surrounding Tieck.

Cross ref.: 57, 684.

## 2. RESEARCH REPORTS

3. Minder, Robert. "Das gewandelte Tieck-Bild." Pp. 181-204 in *Festschrift für Klaus Ziegler*, ed. Eckehard Catholy and Winfried Hellmann. Tübingen: Max Niemeyer, 1968. 473 pp.

    Discusses a few representative contributions to the secondary literature on Tieck with the intention of demonstrating that literary critics have begun to treat Tieck's works more fairly since the turn of the century. See also next two items.

4. ___. "Redécouverte de Tieck." *EG*, 23 (1968): 537-547.

    Argues that German scholars contributed significantly less to the recent Tieck "Renaissance" than their foreign counterparts.

5. ___. "Wandlungen des Tieck-Bildes." Pp. 60-76, 88-90 in *Romantik heute: Friedrich Schlegel, Novalis, E.T.A. Hoffmann, Ludwig Tieck*. Bonn-Bad Godesberg: Inter Nationes, 1972. 94 pp.

    A revised version of no. 3.

6. Paulin, Roger. "Der alte Tieck." Pp. 247-262 in *Zur Literatur der Restaurationsepoche 1815-1848: Forschungs-*

*referate und Aufsätze*, ed. Jost Hermand and Manfred Windfuhr. Stuttgart: J.B. Metzler, 1970. viii + 599 pp.

Surveys the research on Tieck's later novellas and concludes that much remains to be done in order to fully rehabilitate the image of these works.

7. Stopp, E.C. "Wandlungen des Tieckbildes: Ein Literaturbericht." *DVLG*, 17 (1939): 252-276.

Much like the authors of later research reports, Stopp holds Rudolf Haym (no. 93) responsible for having poisoned for generations the critical opinion surrounding Tieck. Most notable is Stopp's diatribe against Zeydel's renowned monograph on Tieck (no. 23), which she attempts to discredit via charges of plagiarism.

8. Thalmann, Marianne. "Hundert Jahre Tieckforschung." *Monatshefte*, 45 (1953): 113-123. Reprinted pp. 63-75 in no. 104.

In very broad strokes, Thalmann summarizes the research on Tieck as conducted in the century following his death and identifies important misconceptions and lacunae therein.

Cross ref.: 88.

# II. Biography

## 1. COMPREHENSIVE OVERVIEWS

9. Baus, Lothar. *Wolfgang Goethes und Uranias Sohn – Ludwig Tieck * ca. 10. März 1773 [offiziell am 31. Mai 1773] † am 28. April 1853: Das Desaster der Germanistik*. Homburg/Saar: Asclepios, 1990. 133 pp.

    A humorous reinterpretation of Tieck's life revolving around the myth that Goethe was Tieck's actual father and wrote all of his "son's" works. Baus subsequently concludes that the distinction traditionally made between German Classicism and Romanticism is a sham.

10. Bernhardi, Wilhelm. "Johann Ludwig Tieck." Pp. 251-276 in *Allgemeine Deutsche Biographie*, Vol. 38, ed. Historische Commission bei der königl. Akademie der Wissenschaften [Bavaria]. Leipzig: Duncker & Humblot, 1894. 796 pp. Reprinted Berlin: Duncker & Humblot, 1971.

    Tieck's life and works as portrayed in a standard biographical compendium.

11. Frank, Manfred. "Johann Ludwig Tieck: 1773-1853." Pp. 246-247 in *Deutsche Schriftsteller im Porträt*, Vol. 3:

*Sturm und Drang, Klassik, Romantik*, ed. Jörn Göres. Beck'sche Schwarze Reihe, Vol. 214. Munich: C.H. Beck, 1980. 287 pp.

Short biographical sketch in a useful reference series.

12. Graef, Hermann. *Johann Ludwig Tieck*. Beiträge zur Literaturgeschichte, Vol. 26. Leipzig: Verlag für Literatur, Kunst und Musik, 1907. 29 pp.

    An extremely positive, but uncritical, view of Tieck's life. Outdated.

13. Günzel, Klaus. *König der Romantik: Das Leben des Dichters Ludwig Tieck in Briefen, Selbstzeugnissen und Berichten*. Berlin: Verlag der Nation; Tübingen: Rainer Wunderlich Verlag, Hermann Leins, 1981. 562 pp.

    This nicely illustrated volume represents a lively supplement to the more traditional life and works approaches to Tieck.

14. Hoeft, Bernhard. *Berühmte Männer und Frauen Berlins und ihre Grabstätten*, Vol. 1. Berlin: Georg Siemens, 1919. iv + 223 pp.

    Pp. 35-43 contain a brief overview of Tieck's life and a photograph of his headstone located at the Dreifaltigkeitsfriedhof in Berlin.

15. Köpke, Rudolf. *Ludwig Tieck: Erinnerungen aus dem Leben des Dichters nach dessen mündlichen und schriftlichen Mittheilungen*. 2 Vols. Leipzig: F.A. Brockhaus, 1855. xxvi + 384, viii + 314 pp. Reprinted Darmstadt: Wissenschaftliche Buchgesellschaft, 1970.

    Compiled by Tieck's "Eckermann," this treasure trove of source material is marred by occasional inaccuracies and trivial anecdotes. Still indispensible despite the existence of much more critical and up-to-date biographies (see nos. 17,

21, 23, 24, and especially no. 20). Concerning the production of the present item, see nos. 78 and 79.

16. Maione, Italo. *Profili della Germanica romantica: Fr. Schlegel, Novalis, Schleiermacher, Tieck, Wackenroder*, 2nd ed. Naples: Libreria Scientifica Editrice, 1960. 301 pp.

   The most comprehensive survey of Tieck's life and works available in the Italian language can be found on pp. 213-268.

17. Minder, Robert. *Un poète romantique allemand: Ludwig Tieck (1773-1853)*. Publications de la Faculté des Lettres de l'Université de Strasbourg, Vol. 72. Paris: Les Belles Lettres, 1936. viii + 517 pp.

   A detailed and critical life and works treatment with a distinct psychological bent. Provides unique insight into the various forces shaping Tieck's romantic nature. Along with no. 23, this monograph provided a great deal of impetus for the modern rediscovery of Tieck. However, it has largely been eclipsed by no. 20.

18. ___. "Ludwig Tieck." Pp. 166-177 in *Le Romantisme allemand: Textes et études*, ed. Albert Béguin, 2nd ed. [Paris]: Les Cahiers du Sud, 1949. 493 pp. Translated by Minder as "Ludwig Tieck, ein Porträt," pp. 266-278 in no. 88.

   Little more than a summary of the preceding item, this article ends on a rather sour note, particularly in its German version, where Tieck is stamped a "Geist zweiten Ranges" for his apparent failure to make a clean break with literary tradition.

19. Neunzig, Hans A. "Ludwig Tieck." Pp. 53-93 in Neunzig, *Lebensläufe der deutschen Romantik: Schriftsteller*. Munich: Kindler, 1986. 287 pp.

An informative, modern, and well-written biographical sketch that could be recommended to students.

20. Paulin, Roger. *Ludwig Tieck: A Literary Biography*. Oxford: Clarendon Press, 1985. xiv + 434 pp. Translated by Hannelore Faden as *Ludwig Tieck: Eine literarische Biographie*. Munich: C.H. Beck, 1988. 350 pp.

The definitive biography. This thorough, critical, and carefully researched examination of Tieck's life and works goes to lengths not only to dispel many of the misconceptions surrounding Tieck's often controversial existence, but also to add new material to the documentary base concerning this author and his times.

21. Rek, Klaus. *Das Dichterleben des Ludwig Tieck: Biographie*. Berlin: Unabhängige Verlagsbuchhandlung Ackerstraße, 1991. 187 pp.

Much like no. 24, this monograph is an attempt at creating a homegrown German biography of Tieck – something which has not existed, at least not in book-length form, since Köpke (no. 15). Generally speaking, it lacks the penetration of Paulin's study (preceding item) which, ironically, is available in German. Includes a collection of "Zeugnisse von Zeitgenossen," a chronology of Tieck's life, and numerous illustrations.

22. Schack, Adolf Friedrich Graf von. "Ludwig Tieck." Pp. 34-39 in Schack, *Episteln und Elegieen*. Stuttgart: J.G. Cotta, 1894. viii + 233 pp.

A summary of Tieck's life and major literary achievements in verse form.

23. Zeydel, Edwin H. *Ludwig Tieck, the German Romanticist: A Critical Study*. Princeton: Princeton University Press, 1935. xvi + 406 pp. Reprinted Hildesheim, New York: Georg Olms, 1971.

This fact-filled critical appraisal of Tieck's life and works was the undisputed English-language standard-bearer until the appearance of no. 20. Still worth consulting, however, particularly concerning Tieck's relations with his German and foreign contemporaries.

24. Ziegener, Thomas. *Ludwig Tieck: Proteus, Pumpgenie und Erzpoet. Leben und Werke*. Frankfurt am Main: R.G. Fischer, 1990. 191 pp.

    Tieck's "dialogische Natur" represents the cornerstone of this work, which is similar to no. 21 in that it intends to break the foreign hegemony over Tieck's biography. But it is too narrow in scope to eclipse its predecessors. Includes a chronology of Tieck's life.

Cross ref.: 2, 80, 688.

## 2. SPECIFIC ASPECTS OF TIECK'S LIFE

### a. Childhood, Years of Study and Travel (1773-1819)

25. Brinker-Gabler, Gisela. "Tieck und die Wissenschaft." *JFDH*, 1976, pp. 168-177.

    On Tieck's unsuccessful bid for a professorship at the University of Heidelberg in 1804.

26. Cohn, Alfons Fedor. "Ludwig Tieck's Reise nach London und Paris im Jahre 1817: Aus Wilhelm von Burgsdorffs Tagebuch." *Zeitschrift für Bücherfreunde*, N.S. 1 (1910): 343-364.

    A travelogue based on the rather careless diary entries of Tieck's longtime friend and traveling companion.

27. Fränkel, Ludwig. "L. Tieck in Weimar 1793." *Goethe-Jahrbuch*, 16 (1895): 200-201.

   Quotes passages relating to Weimar from a previously unpublished letter written by Tieck to his sister Sophie (see no. 474) concerning his trip from Berlin to Erlangen.

28. Gillies, A. "Ludwig Tieck's English Studies at the University of Göttingen, 1792-1794." *JEGP*, 36 (1937): 206-223.

   Focuses primarily on the English-language books checked out by Tieck at the University of Göttingen library.

29. ___. "Ludwig Tieck's Initiation into Spanish Studies." *MLR*, 33 (1938): 396-401.

   Thomas Christian Tychsen, Professor at Göttingen, was Tieck's first teacher of Spanish.

30. Hölter, Achim. "Der Romantiker als Student: Zur Identität von zwei Tieck-Handschriften." *DVLG*, 61 (1987): 125-150.

   Identifies two manuscripts from Tieck's university years as lecture notes taken in courses dealing with classical literature and civilization.

31. Kröll, Joachim. "Ludwig Tieck und Wilhelm Heinrich Wackenroder in Franken." *Archiv für die Geschichte von Oberfranken*, 41 (1961): 345-377.

   Based on a letter from Tieck to Bernhardi dated 1793 (see no. 535), in which he details his travels through Franconia with Wackenroder.

32. Stadelmann, Rudolf and Wolfram Fischer. "Johann Ludwig Tieck aus Berlin: Der Aufgeklärte." Pp. 139-143 in Stadelmann and Fischer, *Die Bildungswelt des deutschen Handwerkers um 1800: Studien zur Soziologie des*

*Kleinbürgers im Zeitalter Goethes.* Berlin: Duncker & Humblot, 1955. 258 pp.

On Tieck's parents, his family history, and especially the social milieu in which he grew up.

33. Trainer, James. "Tieck, Rambach and the Corruption of Young Genius." *GL&L*, N.S. 16 (1962): 27-35.

    Tieck's beginnings as an author were greatly influenced - or, as Trainer contends - corrupted by his mentors August Ferdinand Bernhardi and Friedrich Eberhard Rambach.

Cross ref.: 670.

### b. Years in Dresden, "Vorleseabende" (1819-1841)

34. Beutel, Georg. "Tiecks Vorlesungen in Dresden." *Dresdner Geschichtsblätter*, 22, No. 4 (1913): 57-68.

    A trivial account based on secondhand information.

35. Blaze [de Bury], Henri. "Louis Tieck." Pp. 363-370 in Blaze, *Écrivains et poètes de l'Allemagne.* Paris: Michel Lévy Frères, 1846. 426 pp.

    Introduces Tieck's famous "Vorleseabende" to the French reading public via a report by Carus (next item).

36. Carus, C.G. "Ludwig Tieck: Zur Geschichte seiner Vorlesungen in Dresden." *Historisches Taschenbuch*, N.S. 6 (1845): 193-238.

    Like nos. 41, 43, 44, 46, and 64, an eyewitness account of the "Vorleseabende," stemming here from a noted Goethe scholar and physiognomist.

37. Eulenberg, Herbert. "Ludwig Tieck." *Freie Deutsche Bühne*, 1 (1919): 16-21.

Tieck's "Vorleseabende" from a fictional perspective. Of no scholarly value.

38. ___. "Tieck-Anekdoten." Pp. 98-106 in Eulenberg, *Gestalten und Begebenheiten*. Dresden: Carl Reißner, 1924. 284 pp.

    Trivial anecdotes from Tieck's Dresden period.

39. Freiberg, Günther von. "Phantasus." *Über Land und Meer*, 43 (1880): 351-354.

    Life at the Tieck household in Dresden. A sentimental tribute.

40. Friesen, Hermann Freiherr von. *Ludwig Tieck: Erinnerungen eines alten Freundes aus den Jahren 1825-1842*. 2 Vols. Vienna: Wilhelm Braumüller, 1871. x + 256, 367 pp.

    A highly subjective commentary on the Dresden years that is often of doubtful credibility.

41. Hahn, R.E. "Ein Abend bei Ludwig Tieck." *Über Land und Meer*, 10 (1863): 436, 438, 451-453.

    Firsthand impressions of the "Vorleseabende" à la nos. 36, 43, 44, 46, and 64.

42. Paulin, Roger. "'Höfisches Biedermeier': Ludwig Tieck und der Dresdner Hof. Mit einem unveröffentlichten Brief Ludwig Tiecks an König Friedrich August II. von Sachsen." Pp. 207-227 in *Literatur in der sozialen Bewegung: Aufsätze und Forschungsberichte zum 19. Jahrhundert*, ed. Alberto Martino. Tübingen: Max Niemeyer, 1977. 542 pp.

    A critical analysis of Tieck's not always unproblematical dealings with the royal court in Dresden, especially in light of his activities at the royal theater. Provides unique insight into the social and political climate in which Tieck wrote the majority of his later works.

43. Różycki, K. von. "Ein Besuch bei Joh. Friedr. Kind und Ludwig Tieck (1829): Aus Briefen des Anton Ed. Odyniec." *Zeitschrift für Bücherfreunde*, N.S. 2 (1911): 228-231.

Quotes from letters by the minor Polish author Odyniec concerning his visits to the Dresden residences of Kind and Tieck. Firsthand impressions gained at one of Tieck's "Vorleseabende" are included (see also nos. 36, 41, 44, 46, and 64).

44. Scherer, G. "Ein Abend bei Ludwig Tieck." *Europa: Chronik der gebildeten Welt*, 4 (1839): 8-18.

This article differs from the other eyewitness accounts of Tieck's "Vorleseabende" (nos. 36, 41, 43, 46, and 64) in that it is spiced with humorous commentary on the often rather odd mix of people in attendance.

45. Stern, Adolf. "Ludwig Tieck in Dresden." Pp. 1-44 in Stern, *Zur Literatur der Gegenwart: Bilder und Studien*. Leipzig: Bernhard Schlicke, 1880. 267 pp.

Portrays Tieck as the sole source of cultural and intellectual life in Dresden during his stay there from 1819-1841.

46. Sternberg, A. von. "Tieck's Vorlese-Abende in Dresden." *Die Gartenlaube*, 9 (1861): 116-117.

A rather unflattering account despite the fact that Tieck's talent for reading aloud is highly praised (see also nos. 36, 41, 43, 44, and 64).

47. Weller, Maximilian. "Ludwig Tieck (1773-1853)." Pp. 28-77 in Weller, *Die fünf großen Dramenvorleser: Zur Stilkunde und Kulturgeschichte des deutschen Dichtungsvortrags von 1800-1880*. Würzburg-Aumühle: Konrad Triltsch, [1939]. vii + 280 pp.

Traces Tieck's penchant for reading literature aloud from his earliest school days to his last years in Berlin, but emphasizes the "Vorleseabende" in Dresden. For more on Tieck's literature readings in Berlin, see no. 49.

### c. Years in Berlin, Death, and Funeral (1841-1853)

48. Fischer, L.H. *Aus Berlins Vergangenheit: Gesammelte Aufsätze zur Kultur- und Litteraturgeschichte Berlins*. Berlin: Oehmigke, 1891. iv + 205 pp.

    Contains essays on Tieck's relations with the court of Friedrich Wilhelm IV. (pp. 107-141), his activities at the royal theater in Berlin (pp. 96-107, 141-160), his contacts with Adam Oehlenschläger (pp. 162-168) and Justinus Kerner (pp. 180-191), and the role of dreams and visions in his life and works (pp. 168-180). Includes unpublished correspondence between Tieck and numerous individuals at the Berlin court.

49. Pietsch, Ludwig. "Ein Abend bei Ludwig Tieck." *Aurora*, 4 (1934): 99-101.

    Reprinted from an obscure newspaper source dating back to the 1860's, this article deals with Tieck's literature readings in Berlin (see also no. 47).

50. Rellstab, L. "Ludwig Tieck." *Beilage zur Allgemeinen Zeitung*, Munich, 30 April 1853, pp. 1929-1930.

    Summarizes Tieck's last years.

51. Sivers, Jegor von. "Erinnerungen an Ludwig Tieck, aus dessen letztem Lebensjahre." *Belletristische Blätter aus Russland: Aus dem Feuilleton der St. Petersburger Zeitung*, 3 (1855): 239-247.

    A report by a Russian writer who frequently visited Tieck in the last year of his life. Includes anecdotes told by the ailing Tieck, a description of the room in which he died, and commentary on his funeral as well as on the eulogy by A. Sydow (see no. 53 for eulogy text).

52. Stahr, Adolf. "Ludwig Tieck." Pp. 295-308 in Stahr, *Kleine Schriften zur Litteratur und Kunst*, Vol. 1. Berlin: J. Guttentag, 1871. vi + 536 pp.

Some general observations concerning Tieck's life are paired with an account of his funeral in Berlin.

53. Sydow, A. *Worte am Sarge Ludwig Tiecks: Gesprochen am 1. Mai 1853*. Berlin: F. Schulze, 1853. 14 pp.

The eulogy by the "Prediger der neuen Kirche zu Berlin."

54. Zeising, Adolf. "Meister Ludwig Tieck's Heimgang: Novelle." Frankfurt am Main: Meidinger, 1854. 146 pp.

Tieck's last years in Berlin as portrayed in an obscure biographical novella.

### d. Tieck's Library and Literary Remains

55. *Catalogue de la bibliothèque célèbre de M. Ludwig Tieck qui sera vendue à Berlin le 10. Décembre 1849 et jours suivants par MM. A. Asher & Comp*. Berlin: Trowetzsch, 1849. 362 pp. Reprinted Niederwalluf bei Wiesbaden: Dr. Martin Sändig oHG, 1970.

An auction catalog containing 7,930 items, of which those on pp. 196-211 (primarily Americana) did not stem from Tieck's library. Important for scholarship because it demonstrates the enormous range of Tieck's bibliophilic and literary interests.

56. Hauffen, Adolf. "Ludwig Tieck's Nachlaß." *Archiv für Literaturgeschichte*, 15 (1887): 316-322.

Describes the contents of the Tieck archive at the Staatsbibliothek Preußischer Kulturbesitz in Berlin. Largely made up of unpublished early writings. See also next item.

57. Hölter, Achim. *Ludwig Tieck: Literaturgeschichte als Poesie*. Beihefte zum *Euphorion*, Vol. 24. Heidelberg: Carl Winter, 1989. viii + 514 pp.

In a series of appendices, this study contains a listing (with exact library locations cited) of Tieck's yet unpublished literary remains (works, letters, notes, legal documents, and lists) as well as a full bibliography of his published writings (compare with no. 2), a bibliography of contemporary reviews of his works, and a useful selection of secondary sources. The body of the study is devoted to the thesis that, since literary history so pervades all aspects of Tieck's oeuvre, no real distinction can be made between his literary works on the one hand, and his critical and historical writings on the other.

58. Zeydel, Edwin H. "Ludwig Tieck's Library." *MLN*, 42 (1927): 21-25.

A brief overview of Tieck's extensive book collection numbering as many as 36,000 volumes, a portion of which was sold via no. 55 in 1849.

Cross ref.: 169, 670.


### e. Relations with Individuals

*i*. American and British
(Bannatyne, Coleridge, W. Irving, H.C. Robinson, Ticknor)

59. Marquardt, Hertha. *Henry Crabb Robinson und seine deutschen Freunde: Brücke zwischen England und Deutschland im Zeitalter der Romantik*. Palaestra, Vols. 237 and 249. Göttingen: Vandenhoeck & Ruprecht, 1964 and 1967. 368, 608 pp.

Both volumes contain extensive information on the contacts between Tieck and Robinson throughout (see also next item).

60. Mason, Eudo C. *Deutsche und englische Romantik: Eine Gegenüberstellung.* Kleine Vandenhoeck-Reihe, Vol. 85. Göttingen: Vandenhoeck & Ruprecht, 1959. 103 pp.

    Pp. 30-43 of this eminently useful study are devoted to Tieck's relations with Coleridge and Henry Crabbe Robinson. See also preceding item for more on Tieck and Robinson, and nos. 62 and 63 for additional information on Tieck and Coleridge.

61. Trainer, James. "A Scottish Visitor to Ludwig Tieck." *MLR*, 53 (1958): 416-417.

    Identifies Tieck's Scottish visitor in 1819 as the lawyer Andrew Bannatyne, whom Tieck had erroneously named Damatyne in a letter printed in no. 491.

62. Wheeler, Kathleen. "Coleridge's Friendship with Ludwig Tieck." Pp. 96-112 in *New Approaches to Coleridge: Biographical and Critical Essays*, ed. Donald Sultana. Critical Studies Series. London: Vision; Totowa, N.J.: Barnes & Noble, 1981. 264 pp.

    Elaborates on nos. 60 and 63.

63. Willoughby, L.A. "Coleridge and his German Contemporaries." *PEGS*, N.S. 10 (1934): 43-62.

    As far as Tieck is concerned, not as informative as nos. 60 and 62.

64. Zeydel, Edwin H. "George Ticknor and Tieck." *PMLA*, 44 (1929): 879-891.

    This essay on Tieck's friendship with the American Hispanicist George Ticknor focuses in large part on Ticknor's frequent visits to the Tieck household during his 1835-1836 stay in Dresden. Includes Ticknor's appreciative commentary on the famous "Vorleseabende," many of which he attended. For more firsthand accounts of Tieck's literature readings in Dresden, see nos. 36, 41, 43, 44, and 46.

65. ___. "Washington Irving and Ludwig Tieck." *PMLA*, 46 (1931): 946-947.

A note on Irving's brief stay at Tieck's Dresden home in 1823.

Cross ref.: 660, 670.

*ii*. Austrian and German
(Eichendorff, Freytag, Grillparzer, Mörike, Raumer, the Schlegels, Dorothea Tieck, Rahel Varnhagen)

66. Bock, Alfred. "Ludwig Tieck und Gustav Freytag." *Beilage zur Allgemeinen Zeitung*, Munich, 7 January 1896, pp. 4-6.

On Freytag's encounter with Tieck in 1847 and the ensuing friendship between the two writers.

67. Krauß, Rudolf. "Tieck und Mörike." *Beilage zur Allgemeinen Zeitung*, Munich, 29 June 1893, pp. 4-6.

Tieck corresponded with Eduard Mörike, but never met him in person.

68. Matenko, Percy. "Ludwig Tieck and Rahel Varnhagen: A Re-Examination." *Publications of the Leo Baeck Institute*, 20 (1975): 225-246.

Chronicles the relations between Tieck and Rahel primarily via a study of their correspondence.

69. Reinhard, Ewald. "Ludwig Tieck: Zu seinem hundertsten Todestage." *Aurora*, 14 (1954): 98-103.

A note on Tieck's life and works, with special emphasis on his contacts with Joseph von Eichendorff.

70. Stricker, Käthe. "Ihres Vaters Tochter! Dorothea Tieck zum Gedächtnis." *Die Frau*, 43 (1935): 103-112.

Contains information on the relationship between Tieck and his daughter Dorothea, who actively shared his interest in the translation of Shakespeare (see no. 605).

71. Zeydel, Edwin H. "Die ersten Beziehungen Ludwig Tiecks zu den Brüdern Schlegel." *JEGP*, 27 (1928): 16-41, 383-386.

Tieck's early relations with the Schlegels tended to be problematical, especially in the case of Friedrich. Pp. 383-386 represent an addendum to this article.

72. ___. "Ludwig Tieck and Friedrich von Raumer." *PMLA*, 43 (1928): 863-893.

This essay on the friendship between Tieck and the noted Berlin historian is based largely on their extant correspondence (see nos. 507-510).

73. ___. "Tieck und Grillparzer." *GRM*, 24 (1936): 372-379.

Utilizing unpublished source materials, Zeydel illustrates the antipathy that existed between the two poets.

Cross ref.: 48 (Kerner).

*iii.* Danish
(Oehlenschläger)

74. Sergel, Albert. "Oehlenschläger und Tieck." Pp. 44-67 in Sergel, *Oehlenschläger in seinen persönlichen Beziehungen zu Goethe, Tieck und Hebbel: Nebst einer Oehlenschläger-Bibliographie*. Rostock: C.J.E. Volckmann Nachfolger, 1907. 144 pp.

A detailed account of Tieck's friendship with the Danish romanticist drawing on a wealth of source material. Contains a previously unpublished letter from Tieck to Oehlenschläger written in July of 1820.

Cross ref.: 48, 637.

### iv. French and Russian

75. Lambert, José. "Tieck, ses visiteurs et ses correspondants français." *RLC*, 44 (1970): 56-72.

    Tieck's contacts with such French luminaries as Ampère, Marmier, Montalembert, David d'Angers, Mme. de Staël, and Balzac.

76. Matenko, Percy. "Tieck's Russian Friends." *PMLA*, 55 (1940): 1129-1145.

    On Tieck's relations with Zhukovski, Küchelbecker, and other prominent Russians.

### 3. MISCELLANEOUS

77. Hoffner, Wilhelm. "Phantastische Gesichtserscheinungen von Goethe, Tieck und Otto Ludwig." *Westermann's Jahrbuch der Illustrirten Deutschen Monatshefte*, 20 (1866): 258-265.

    A collection of trivial anecdotes from the lives of Goethe, Tieck, and Ludwig concerning literary inspiration and production. Of little scholarly value.

78. Kanzog, Klaus. "Rudolf Köpkes handschriftliche Aufzeichnungen der Kleist-Bemerkungen Tiecks: Zugleich ein Schlußwort zur Manuskript-Lage des *Prinz von Homburg*." *Euphorion*, 62 (1968): 160-168.

Demonstrates via information concerning Heinrich von Kleist that Köpke, when writing his Tieck biography (no. 15), did not always remain faithful to his interview notes.

79. ___. "Ratschläge Friedrich von Raumers zur Tieck-Biographie Rudolf Köpkes." *JFDH*, 1970, pp. 203-225.

Uses hitherto unpublished letters and notes to document Friedrich von Raumer's influence on the preparation of no. 15.

80. Schweikert, Uwe. "Eduard von Bülow: Aufzeichnungen über Ludwig Tieck." *JFDH*, 1972, pp. 318-368.

First publication and critical analysis of notes written by Tieck's friend and literary collaborator Eduard von Bülow for his planned biography on Tieck, which never materialized. Based for the most part on conversations between the two men, these notes range in topic from Tieck's youth to his later years in Dresden and Berlin, but lack any sort of organization.

81. Zeydel, Edwin H. "A Note on Ludwig Tieck." *PQ*, 6, No. 4 (1927): 80-83.

Comments on the dearth of truly critical Tieck biographies and points out various inaccuracies in existing scholarship surrounding Tieck's life and works. A prelude to no. 23.

# III. Criticism: General

## 1. GENERAL INTRODUCTIONS TO TIECK'S OEUVRE

82. Alewyn, Richard. "Ludwig Tieck." Pp. 96-101 in Alewyn, *Probleme und Gestalten: Essays*. Frankfurt am Main: Insel, 1974. 403 pp.

    Superficial by contrast to other introductions in this section.

83. Gumbel, Hermann. "Ludwig Tiecks dichterischer Weg." Pp. 63-82 in Gumbel et al, *Romantik-Forschungen. DVLG* Buchreihe, Vol. 16. Halle a. d. Saale: Max Niemeyer, 1929. v + 333 pp. Reprinted pp. 172-190 in no. 88.

    A psychologically-oriented overview emphasizing the different literary means employed by Tieck throughout his life in the transcendence of reality.

84. Hoffmann, J.L. "Ludwig Tieck: Eine literarhistorische Skizze." *Album des literarischen Vereins in Nürnberg*, 1856, pp. 1-80.

    Highly appreciative, but largely outdated. With plot summaries and short interpretations.

85. Kern, Johannes P. *Ludwig Tieck: Dichter einer Krise*. Poesie und Wissenschaft, Vol. 18. Heidelberg: Lothar Stiehm, 1977. 236 pp.

   Heavily indebted to the sympathetic Tieck scholarship of Marianne Thalmann. Good interpretations.

86. Klussmann, Paul Gerhard. "Ludwig Tieck." Pp. 15-52 in *Deutsche Dichter des 19. Jahrhunderts: Ihr Leben und Werk*, ed. Benno von Wiese. Berlin: Erich Schmidt, 1969. 600 pp.

   Extends beyond a mere overview to correct the misconceptions and biases expressed vis-à-vis Tieck in nos. 92, 93, and 101.

87. Ribbat, Ernst. *Ludwig Tieck: Studien zur Konzeption und Praxis romantischer Poesie*. Kronberg/Ts.: Athenäum, 1978. 290 pp.

   One of the best and most comprehensive introductions to all phases of Tieck's output. Includes interpretations, a discussion of Tieck's image in Germany, and a lengthy bibliography.

88. Segebrecht, Wulf, ed. *Ludwig Tieck*. Wege der Forschung, Vol. 386. Darmstadt: Wissenschaftliche Buchgesellschaft, 1976. xxix + 471 pp.

   Comprised of nos. 18, 83, 92, 100, 101, 112, 157, 247, 276, 317, 360, and 377. Segebrecht's introductory essay (pp. vii-xxix) represents a useful research report.

89. Trainer, James. "Ludwig Tieck." Pp. 39-57 in *German Men of Letters*, Vol. 1, ed. Alex Natan, 2nd ed. London: Oswald Wolff, 1965. viii + 273 pp.

   Ideal for students.

## 2. TIECK AS ROMANTIC AUTHOR

90. Brion, Marcel. "Ludwig Tieck." Pp. 229-298, 353-355 in Brion, *L'Allemagne romantique: Kleist, Brentano, Wackenroder, Tieck, Caroline von Günderode*, Vol. 1. Paris: Albin Michel, 1962. 363 pp.

   In this ambivalent study, Brion claims to see no artistic development within the body of Tieck's romantic work.

91. Croce, Elena Craveri. "Due Scrittori tedeschi." *Quaderni della "Critica,"* 7 (1951): 112-143.

   Appreciative essays introducing the romantic works of Tieck (pp. 112-134) and Chamisso (pp. 134-143) to an Italian audience.

92. Gundolf, Friedrich. "Ludwig Tieck." *JFDH*, 1929, pp. 99-195. Reprinted pp. 1-139 in Gundolf, *Romantiker: Neue Folge*, Berlin-Wilmersdorf: H. Keller, 1931. 255 pp. And pp. 191-265 in no. 88.

   Repeats many of Rudolf Haym's prejudices (see next item) by characterizing the romantic Tieck as a superficial, unoriginal, and careless writer who never really overcame his beginnings as a hack.

93. Haym, Rudolf. *Die romantische Schule: Ein Beitrag zur Geschichte des deutschen Geistes*. Berlin: Rudolph Gaertner, 1870. 951 pp. Reprinted Darmstadt: Wissenschaftliche Buchgesellschaft, 1961.

   Scattered throughout this volume is perhaps the most influential commentary ever composed on the romantic Tieck. Through its misconceptions and biases, this work has succeeded in placing not only Tieck's talent and originality as an author in serious question, but his integrity as an individual as well. Although modern critics have made a concerted effort to undo the damage inflicted by Haym, we can still find echoes of his way of thinking in recent publications (see next item, for example).

94. Hillmann, Heinz. "Ludwig Tieck." Pp. 114-138 in *Deutsche Dichter der Romantik: Ihr Leben und Werk*, ed. Benno von Wiese, 2nd. ed. Berlin: Erich Schmidt, 1983. 659 pp.

Reverberations of Haym (preceding item) fill this depressing portrayal, in which Tieck's lifelong financial difficulties are blamed for a perceived fixation on money in his romantic writings.

95. Kasack, Hermann. "Die Gefährten: Ludwig Tieck." Pp. 54-69 in Kasack, *Mosaiksteine: Beiträge zu Literatur und Kunst*. Frankfurt am Main: Suhrkamp, 1956. 413 pp.

Views Tieck's literary achievements primarily in relation to those of his German romantic contemporaries.

96. Kausler, Rudolph. "Ludwig Tieck und die deutsche Romantik: Historische Skizze." *Der Freihafen*, 2, No. 3 (1839): 106-139; and No. 4 (1839): 74-105.

A surprisingly positive overview considering Kausler's ties to Young Germany, whose antagonistic stance towards Romanticism in general, and towards Tieck in particular, is legendary.

97. Lieske, Rudolf. *Tiecks Abwendung von der Romantik*. Germanistische Studien, Vol. 134. Berlin: Emil Ebering, 1933. 150 pp.

Contends that, after enduring a "Seelenkrise" brought about by the realization that he could never be "ganz Romantiker und Mystiker wie Novalis" as well as after the failure of his romantic poetry and drama, Tieck turned away from Romanticism to embrace a largely realistic view of life in his later novellas – although the latter still contain a few "romantische oder poetische Ausschmückungen." A well-written and influential study that is not without its serious detractors (see especially nos. 149, 150, and 354).

98. Lussky, Alfred Edwin. *Tieck's Approach to Romanticism.* Borna-Leipzig: Robert Noske, 1925. x + 119 pp.

Tieck was "by nature of a romantic turn of mind" – a conclusion contradicting Haym (no. 93) and Koldewey (no. 109), who state that Tieck's Romanticism, little more than an affectation, was derived from Wackenroder.

99. Paulin, Roger. "The Early Ludwig Tieck and the Idyllic Tradition." *MLR*, 70 (1975): 110-124.

The transition from Enlightenment to Romanticism is clearly marked in Tieck's oeuvre by the gradual dissipation of idyllic elements (see also no. 435). Unpublished archival materials are utilized in support of this thesis.

100. Rosenkranz, Karl. "Ludwig Tieck und die romantische Schule." *Hallische Jahrbücher für deutsche Wissenschaft und Kunst*, 1 (1838): Cols. 1233-1235, 1241-1243, 1249-1253, 1257-1260, 1273-1278, 1281-1302. Reprinted pp. 1-44 in no. 88.

A well-written, insightful, but largely forgotten introduction to the early works of Tieck and their place within German Romanticism. Makes the important observation that Tieck is "der Mittelpunkt der romantischen Schule; seine Geschichte ist ihre Geschichte und umgekehrt."

101. Staiger, Emil. "Ludwig Tieck und der Ursprung der deutschen Romantik." Pp. 175-204 in Staiger, *Stilwandel: Studien zur Vorgeschichte der Goethezeit.* Zurich, Freiburg i. Br.: Atlantis, 1963. 204 pp. Reprinted pp. 322-351 in no. 88.

Even though he credits Tieck with having fathered German Romanticism, Staiger writes him off as a superficial and uncritical author, thereby repeating much of what is said in nos. 92 and 93.

102. Tecchi, Bonaventura. "Ritratto di Tieck (nel I centenario della morte)." Pp. 1-47 in Tecchi, *Romantici tedeschi*, 2nd ed. Milan, Naples: Riccardo Ricciardi, 1964. vii + 225 pp.

This general overview of Tieck's romantic writings includes a bibliography of Italian Tieck translations.

103. Thalmann, Marianne. *Ludwig Tieck: Der romantische Weltmann aus Berlin*. Dalp-Taschenbücher, Vol. 318. Berne: Francke; Munich: Lehnen, 1955. 144 pp.

In this treatment of Tieck's early works, Thalmann succeeds in defining – with more accuracy than most other critics – exactly what makes Tieck the quintessential German romantic.

104. ___. *Romantik in kritischer Perspektive: Zehn Studien*, ed. Jack D. Zipes. Poesie und Wissenschaft, Vol. 20. Heidelberg: Lothar Stiehm, 1976. 201 pp.

A selection from Thalmann's previously published articles on German Romanticism, including nos. 8, 126, 148, and 198 devoted to Tieck. With an introduction by Zipes and a complete Thalmann bibliography.

105. Wernaer, Robert M. *Romanticism and the Romantic School in Germany*. New York, London: D. Appleton, 1910. xv + 373 pp. Reprinted New York: Haskell House, 1966.

Included here because it still represents one of the best English-language introductions to German Romanticism in general and to Tieck in particular. See especially Ch. 7: "Tieck as a Representative of the Romantic Mood" (pp. 108-130).

106. Zeydel, Edwin H. "A Note on Tieck's Early Romanticism." *MLN*, 41 (1926): 444-449.

Quotes from previously published letters by Tieck to demonstrate that he was of an inherently romantic nature.

Cross ref.: 256.

## 3. SOURCES FOR TIECK'S WORKS

### a. German

107. Ederheimer, Edgar. *Jakob Boehmes Einfluß auf Ludwig Tieck*. Heidelberg: Carl Winter, 1904. 56 pp.

    Traces of Böhme's mysticism can be found throughout Tiecks oeuvre. Includes a summary of Böhme's teachings. See also nos. 329, 330, and 340.

108. Görte, Erna. *Der junge Tieck und die Aufklärung*. Germanistische Studien, Vol. 45. Berlin: Emil Ebering, 1926. 102 pp.

    The influence of Wolff, Kant, Fichte, Nicolai, Moses Mendelssohn, Lessing, Sulzer, Gottsched, Moritz, and others on Tieck's early works.

109. Koldewey, Paul. *Wackenroder und sein Einfluß auf Tieck*. Altona: Hammerich & Lesser, [1904]. 212 pp.

    Attempts to diminish Tieck's talent and originality as an author by claiming that his romantic writings were totally indebted to Wackenroder (compare with nos. 93 and 98). See also nos. 626-632.

110. Minor, Jacob. "Classiker und Romantiker." *Goethe-Jahrbuch*, 10 (1889): 212-232.

    Deals with the impact of Goethe and Schiller on the works of Tieck and his romantic contemporaries. Also shows how

Tieck's *Octavianus* influenced Goethe's *Faust*. For more on Tieck and Goethe, see nos. 111, 112, 176, 237, 443, 690, and 691. More on Tieck and Schiller can be found in nos. 692-694.

111. Ribbat, Ernst. "Ungleichzeitig-Gleichzeitig: Goethe und Tieck." *JIG*, Series A: *Kongreßberichte*, Vol. 8, Part 3 (1980): 339-343.

  Speaks out against the replacement of the term "Goethe-Zeit" by "Tieck-Zeit" as proposed by various critics. Argues that Tieck not only lacks Goethe's immense "Nachruhm," but also – and most importantly – that many of his works would have been unthinkable without his reading and appreciation of Goethe (see also nos. 110, 112, 176, 237, and 443).

112. Thalmann, Marianne. "Tiecks Goethebild." *Monatshefte*, 50 (1958): 225-242. Reprinted pp. 279-302 in no. 88.

  Mostly, Tieck glorified only the pre-Weimar Goethe, who had been a model for the romantic generation in Germany. For additional references to Goethe's influence, see nos. 110, 111, 176, 237, and 443.

Cross ref.: 139, 172, 175, 203, 217, 247, 261, 264-266, 286, 339, 397, 398, 617, 648-650, 719.

**b. Other**

113. Bertrand, J.-J. A. *Cervantes et le romantisme allemand*. Paris: Félix Alcan, 1914. viii + 671 pp.

  As far as Tieck is concerned, discusses Cervantes' influence on *William Lovell, Franz Sternbalds Wanderungen, Prinz Zerbino, Die verkehrte Welt*, and "Der junge Tischlermeister" (see also nos. 114 and 396).

114. Lussky, Alfred E. "Cervantes and Tieck's Idealism." *PMLA*, 43 (1928): 1082-1097.

Tieck's reading of Cervantes' *Don Quixote* in the 1790's awakened his romantic idealism and caused him to break with the rationalism of Friedrich Nicolai, to whose *Straußfedern* he contributed, as well as with the nihilism pervading his own *William Lovell*. For more on Tieck and Cervantes, see nos. 113 and 396.

115. Stopp, Elisabeth. "Ludwig Tieck and Dante." *Deutsches Dante-Jahrbuch*, 60 (1985): 73-95.

   The only extensive treatment of this subject, Stopp's excellent article focuses not only on Dante's role in *Prinz Zerbino* (see no. 212), but also on Tieck's advice regarding the Dante translations of Prince John of Saxony, and on Dante's influence on *Sternbald, Genoveva,* and other works by Tieck.

Cross ref.: 139, 172, 174, 178, 183-188, 207, 216, 218-224, 256, 274, 278, 409, 411, 412, 452, 677.


## 4. TIECK'S WORKS: STYLISTIC ANALYSES

116. Mai, Andrea Angela. "Studien zu Wort und Satz bei Ludwig Tieck." Diss. Munich, 1967.

   A useful general analysis.

117. Petrich, Hermann. *Drei Kapitel vom romantischen Stil: Ein Beitrag zur Charakteristik der romantischen Schule, ihrer Sprache und Dichtung, mit vorwiegender Rücksicht auf Ludwig Tieck.* Leipzig: R. Jenne, 1878. xvi + 152 pp. Reprinted Osnabrück: Zeller, 1964.

   Focuses on "Bildlichkeit," "Archaismus," and "Mystik" within Tieck's writing style, primarily vis-à-vis his earlier works.

118. Thalmann, Marianne. *Romantik und Manierismus.* Sprache und Literatur, Vol. 7. Stuttgart: W. Kohlhammer, 1963. 214 pp.

   Contains a general discussion of the mannerism inherent in Tieck's writing style. Supplemented by no. 198.

Cross ref.: 402.


## 5. TIECK'S WORKS: THEMATIC STUDIES

### a. Alienation

119. Hammes, Michael Paul. *"Waldeinsamkeit": Eine Motiv- und Stiluntersuchung zur deutschen Frühromantik, insbesondere zu Ludwig Tieck.* Limburg a. d. Lahn: Limburger Vereinsdruckerei, 1933. 95 pp.

   The motif "Waldeinsamkeit" functions largely as a "Stimmungsfaktor" throughout Tieck's oeuvre.

120. Steindecker, Werner. *Studien zum Motiv des einsamen Menschen bei Novalis und Tieck.* Breslau: Priebatsch, 1937. vii + 81 pp.

   A superficial study that, in the case of Tieck, is limited to his early works.

Cross ref.: 671.


### b. Color, Synaesthetic Imagery

121. Fischer, Ottokar. "Über Verbindung von Farbe und Klang: Eine literar-psychologische Untersuchung." *Zeitschrift für Ästhetik und allgemeine Kunstwissenschaft,* 2 (1907): 501-534.

On the psychological significance of the synaesthetic images employed by Tieck.

122. Haußmann, J.F. "Die optischen Qualitäten in den Jugendwerken Tiecks." *Zeitschrift für Ästhetik und allgemeine Kunstwissenschaft*, 8 (1913): 606-614.

Reports on the frequency with which Tieck uses various colors, but offers no critical evaluation of the findings.

123. Katz, Moritz. *Die Schilderung des musikalischen Eindrucks bei Schumann, Hoffmann und Tieck*. Leipzig: Johann Ambrosius Barth, 1910. 55 pp.

A useless statistical analysis.

124. Rowley, Brian A. "The Light of Music and the Music of Light: Synaesthetic Imagery in the Works of Ludwig Tieck." *PEGS*, 26 (1956/57): 52-80.

Tieck clearly favored visual-for-auditory over auditory-for-visual images.

125. Steinert, Walter. *Ludwig Tieck und das Farbempfinden der romantischen Dichtung*. Schriften der Literarhistorischen Gesellschaft Bonn, Vol. 7. Dortmund: Fr. Wilh. Ruhfus, 1910. vii + 241 pp.

Discusses the interaction between color and light in Tieck's many descriptions of nature (see also no. 140).

126. Thalmann, Marianne. "Formen und Verformen durch die Vergeistigung der Farben." *JWGV*, 68 (1964): 124-148. Reprinted pp. 152-184 in no. 104.

This commentary on the use of color in the works of Tieck and his romantic contemporaries is out of touch with other research on the subject.

Cross ref.: 152.

### c. The Demonic, Fateful, Supernatural

127. Busch, Willi. *Das Element des Dämonischen in Ludwig Tiecks Dichtungen.* Delitzsch: C.A. Walter, 1911. 74 pp.

    Complements no. 130 by covering not only Tieck's earliest writings, but also those from his romantic and realistic periods (see also no. 131).

128. Corkhill, Alan. *The Motif of "Fate" in the Works of Ludwig Tieck.* Stuttgarter Arbeiten zur Germanistik, Vol. 38. Stuttgart: Hans-Dieter Heinz, 1978. 238 pp.

    A study on the philosophical, theological, and psychological dimensions of fate in early works by Tieck. Views the motif of fate as a medium for "artistic continuity" within Tieck's entire output. For more on fate, see nos. 176 and 177.

129. Field, Jean Clark. *Das Wunderbare bei Ludwig Tieck.* Zurich: Ernst Lang, 1939. 119 pp.

    Relates Tieck's concept of the supernatural, as expressed throughout his oeuvre, to his personal weltanschauung and psychic state.

130. Hemmer, Heinrich. *Die Anfänge L. Tiecks und seiner dämonisch-schauerlichen Dichtung.* Acta Germanica, Vol. 6, No. 3. Berlin: Mayer & Müller, 1910. xiii + 212 pp.

    The demonic and gothic elements in pre-1791 works by Tieck are attributed less to his reading of Shakespeare and German Storm and Stress authors than to his alleged psychological imbalances (see also nos. 127 and 131).

131. Thalmann, Marianne. *Probleme der Dämonie in Ludwig Tiecks Schriften.* Forschungen zur neueren Literaturgeschichte, Vol. 53. Weimar: Alexander Duncker, 1919. 101 pp.

Much like Hemmer (preceding item), Thalmann holds Tieck's "seelischer Antagonismus" responsible for the many demonic elements in his oeuvre (see also no. 127).

Cross ref.: 238, 253, 257, 274, 276, 291, 326, 377.

### d. Humor, Satire

132. Brummack, Jürgen. "Ludwig Tieck." Pp. 46-81, 204-209, 231 in Brummack, *Satirische Dichtung: Studien zu Friedrich Schlegel, Tieck, Jean Paul und Heine.* Theorie und Geschichte der Literatur und der schönen Künste, Vol. 53. Munich: Wilhelm Fink, 1979. 239 pp.

Via discussions of *Der gestiefelte Kater,* "Briefe über Shakespeare," and other works, Tieck is characterized as an adept satirist both of the contemporary literary and socio-political scenes.

133. Faerber, Ludwig. *Das Komische bei Ludwig Tieck.* Mainz: Merkel & Köber, 1917. x + 88 pp.

Illuminates the different types of humor employed by Tieck, but concedes that only very few of his writings deserve to be called "komisch" in any traditional sense of the word.

134. Günther, Hans. *Romantische Kritik und Satire bei Ludwig Tieck.* Leipzig: Heinrich Schmidt & Carl Günther, 1907. 213 pp.

A superficial look at Tieck's satirical utterances vis-à-vis the Enlightenment, Classicism, Romanticism, Young Germany, and all forms of popular literature. For a more in-depth approach to this subject, see no. 352.

135. Ribbat, Ernst. "Poesie und Polemik: Zur Entstehungsgeschichte der romantischen Schule und zur Literatursatire Ludwig Tiecks." Pp. 58-79 in *Romantik: Ein literatur-*

*wissenschaftliches Studienbuch*, ed. Ernst Ribbat. Athenäum-Taschenbücher, Vol 2149. Königstein/Ts.: Athenäum, 1979. 236 pp.

Argues that Tieck's satirical works exemplify the romantic generation's struggle to achieve, through its art, social and political "Freiheitsraum" on the one hand, and a "humane Wirklichkeit" on the other.

**e. Incest**

136. Rank, Otto. *Das Inzest-Motiv in Dichtung und Sage: Grundzüge einer Psychologie des dichterischen Schaffens*, 2nd ed. Leipzig, Vienna: Franz Deuticke, 1926. ix + 652 pp. Reprinted Darmstadt: Wissenschaftliche Buchgesellschaft, 1974. Translated by Gregory C. Richter as *The Incest Theme in Literature and Legend: Fundamentals of a Psychology of Literary Creation*. Baltimore: The Johns Hopkins University Press, 1991. 672 pp.

Pp. 566-574 of this groundbreaking survey, which ranges from Oedipus to Ibsen, are devoted to the identification of the incest motif in a variety of earlier writings by Tieck.

137. Trainer, James. "The Incest-Theme in the Works of Tieck." *MLN*, 76 (1961): 819-824.

Expands upon the preceding item by showing that the incest motif not only occurs during Tieck's early phase as a writer, but throughout his entire literary career. Links Tieck's use of the motif to his reception of the Gothic novel instead of to any sort of personal crisis.

Cross ref.: 297, 298, 314.

## f. Irony

138. Budde, Josef. *Zur romantischen Ironie bei Ludwig Tieck*. Bonn: Emil Eisele, 1907. 32 pp.

   A general study lacking clear examples and depth.

139. Lussky, Alfred Edwin. *Tieck's Romantic Irony: With Special Emphasis upon the Influence of Cervantes, Sterne, and Goethe*. Chapel Hill: The University of North Carolina Press, 1932. viii + 274 pp.

   Much more detailed than the preceding item, this monograph focuses primarily on the question of sources. Goes to lengths to distinguish Tieck's concept of irony from that of Friedrich Schlegel.

Cross ref.: 189-193, 201, 204, 206, 215, 404.


## g. Landscape, Nature

140. Danton, George Henry. *The Nature Sense in the Writings of Ludwig Tieck*. New York: The Columbia University Press, 1907. 98 pp. Reprinted New York: AMS Press, 1966.

   Like Steinert (no. 125), Danton stresses the importance of color and light in Tieck's nature descriptions, but offers a more insightful discussion of the symbolic and philosophical significance of these descriptions.

141. Donat, Walter. *Die Landschaft bei Tieck und ihre historischen Voraussetzungen*. Deutsche Forschungen, Vol. 14. Frankfurt am Main: Moritz Diesterweg, 1925. viii + 137 pp.

   On the role of geological formations, vegetation, and the sky within Tieck's nature portrayals.

142. Thalmann, Marianne. *Romantiker entdecken die Stadt.* Sammlung Dialog. Munich: Nymphenburger Verlagshandlung, 1965. 146 pp.

Discusses urban landscapes as presented in the works of Tieck and his romantic contemporaries (see also nos. 410 and 420).

143. Todt, August Wilhelm. *Die Behandlung des Räumlichen bei Tieck.* Darmstadt: K.F. Bender, 1924. 13pp. Excerpt of Diss. Gießen, 1924.

A study on the spatial characteristics of Tieck's oeuvre, with reference to portrayals of both the inside and outside worlds.

Cross ref.: 155, 268, 275, 277, 280, 327, 336, 337, 376, 426, 662.

### h. Society, Social Issues, Artist vs. Society

144. Fritz-Grandjean, Sonia. *Das Frauenbild im Jugendwerk von Ludwig Tieck als Mosaikstein zu seiner Weltanschauung: Essai.* Europäische Hochschulschriften, Series 1: Deutsche Sprache und Literatur, Vol. 320. Berne, Frankfurt am Main, Las Vegas: Peter Lang, 1980. 208 pp.

Women are generally accorded a great deal of status in Tieck's works, particularly from a social standpoint (complements no. 355).

145. Horton, Gudrun. "Die Entstehung des Mittelalterbildes in der deutschen Frühromantik: Wackenroder, Tieck, Novalis und die Brüder Schlegel." *JIG*, Series B: *Germanistische Dissertationen in Kurzfassung*, Vol. 3 (1976): 108-123. Excerpt of Diss. University of Washington, 1973. Abstract in *DAI*, 34, No. 04A (1973): 1858-1859.

Chapter two is devoted to Tieck's image of medieval life and society, which – as manifested in his early literary productions – was shaped primarily by popular eighteenth century attitudes before taking on a more historical and philosophical dimension in his later philological studies.

146. Pikulik, Lothar. *Romantik als Ungenügen an der Normalität: Am Beispiel Tiecks, Hoffmanns, Eichendorffs*. Frankfurt am Main: Suhrkamp, 1979. 550 pp.

Utilizes early works by the named authors to demonstrate that romantic literature represents an escape from the ills of modern society, but that it does not pretend to offer a better way of life (compare with no. 148).

147. Spaulding, John A. "The Lower Middle Class in Tieck's Writings." *JEGP*, 21 (1922): 259-292.

The fact that Tieck consistently drew lower-class characters much more positively than their upper-class brethren attests to the modernity of his oeuvre.

148. Thalmann, Marianne. "'Der unwissend Gläubige': Eine Studie zum Genieproblem." Pp. 105-139 in *On Romanticism and the Art of Translation: Studies in Honor of Edwin Hermann Zeydel*, ed. Gottfried F. Merkel. Princeton: Princeton University Press, 1956. viii + 267 pp. Reprinted pp. 87-115 in no. 104.

In contrast to Pikulik (no. 146), Thalmann argues that escapism is not the motive of the romantic protagonist as found in works by Tieck and others, but rather that he envisions himself as a transcendent "Glaubensheld" who champions the causes of morality, individuality, and humanity in the face of an increasingly bureaucratized and insensitive society.

149. Ziegener, Thomas Günther. *Ludwig Tieck – Studien zur Geselligkeitsproblematik: Die soziologisch-pädagogische Kategorie der Geselligkeit als Einheitsstiftender Faktor in Leben und Werk des Dichters*. Forschungen zur Literatur- und Kulturgeschichte, Vol. 14.

Frankfurt am Main, Berne, New York, Paris: Peter Lang, 1987. 377 pp.

Attempts to disprove the belief that Tieck's works fall into distinct early (romantic) and late (realistic) periods by pointing to the theme of sociability as a constant and thus also unifying factor within Tieck's oeuvre (see also nos. 97, 150, and 354).

Cross ref.: 259, 269, 272, 292, 293, 332, 358, 376, 377, 388, 394, 408, 438, 589.

**i. Other**

150. Hellge, Rosemarie. *Motive und Motivstrukturen bei Ludwig Tieck*. Göppinger Arbeiten zur Germanistik, Vol. 123. Göppingen: Alfred Kümmerle, 1974. 285 pp.

    A general study arriving at the conclusion that Tieck's use of many different motifs remained quite constant throughout his literary career, thus disproving assertions made in no. 97. See also preceding item as well as no. 354.

## 6. MISCELLANEOUS

151. Schweikert, Uwe, ed. *Ludwig Tieck*. Dichter über ihre Dichtungen, Vol. 9. Munich: Heimeran, 1971. 3 vols. 361, 361, 400 pp.

    Tieck's commentary on his own works in the standard series format. An important reference source for the Tieck scholar.

# IV. Criticism: Poetry

## 1. GENERAL

152. Böckmann, Paul. "Klang und Bild in der Stimmungslyrik der Romantik." Pp. 103-125 in *Gegenwart im Geiste: Festschrift für Richard Benz*. Hamburg: Christian Wegner, 1954. 142 pp.

    Through the use of synaesthetic imagery, Tieck paved the way for "die Verwandlung der Erlebnislyrik in die Stimmungslyrik" in Germany. For more on synaesthetic imagery, see nos. 121-126.

153. Erny, Richard. "Entstehung und Bedeutung der romantischen Sprachmusikalität im Hinblick auf Tiecks Verhältnis zur Lyrik." Diss. Heidelberg, 1956.

    An insightful and carefully researched analysis of Tieck's contribution to "romantische Stimmungslyrik" via his musical poems.

154. Gnüg, Hiltrud. *Entstehung und Krise lyrischer Subjektivität: Vom klassischen lyrischen Ich zur modernen Erfahrungswirklichkeit*. Germanistische Ab-

handlungen, Vol. 54. Stuttgart: J.B. Metzler, 1983. viii + 343 pp.

Pp. 94-111 are devoted to a study of melancholy and "Idealitätssehnsucht" in such poems by Tieck as "An denselben" (dedicated to Novalis), "Wie soll ich die Freude," and "Zeit."

155. Greiner, Martin. *Das frühromantische Naturgefühl in der Lyrik von Tieck und Novalis.* Von deutscher Poeterey, Vol. 7. Leipzig: J.J. Weber, 1930. 123 pp.

Describes Tieck's nature poetry as a "Verbreitung über die Oberfläche der Natur" and that of Novalis as a "Drang ins Innere der Natur."

156. Kienzerle, Renate. *Aufbauformen romantischer Lyrik: Aufgezeigt an Tieck, Brentano und Eichendorff.* Ulm-Donau: Karl Höhn, 1946. 144 pp.

Tieck's poems are characterized less by rhyme scheme or strophic structure than by thematic variation.

157. Kluge, Gerhard. "Idealisieren-Poetisieren: Anmerkungen zu poetologischen Begriffen und zur Lyriktheorie des jungen Tieck." *JDSG*, 13 (1969): 308-360. Reprinted pp. 386-443 in no. 88.

Language, feeling, nature, and human existence are all interwoven in an idealized fashion in Tieck's lyrics.

158. Miessner, Wilhelm. *Ludwig Tiecks Lyrik: Eine Untersuchung.* Literarhistorische Forschungen, Vol. 24. Berlin: Emil Felber, 1902. 106 pp. Reprinted Nendeln: Kraus, 1976.

A general thematic study.

159. Neuburger, Paul. *Die Verseinlage in der Prosadichtung der Romantik: Mit einer Einleitung zur Geschichte der Verseinlage.* Palaestra, Vol. 145. Leipzig: Mayer &

Müller, 1924. vii + 332 pp. Reprinted New York, London: Johnson Reprint Co., 1967.

Pp. 127-220 of this important survey deal with verse insertions in Tieck's prose, especially in *William Lovell* and *Franz Sternbalds Wanderungen*. For a discussion of the poems in "Runenberg," see no. 331.

## 2. POEMS FROM THE *GEDICHTE* COLLECTION (1821-1823)

160. Klussmann, Paul Gerhard. "Bewegliche Imagination oder Die Kunst der Töne: Zu Ludwig Tiecks *Glosse*." Pp. 343-357 in *Gedichte und Interpretationen*, Vol. 3: *Klassik und Romantik*, ed. Wulf Segebrecht. Reclams Universal-Bibliothek, Vol. 7892. Stuttgart: Philipp Reclam jun., 1984. 464 pp.

An interpretation of a poem written in 1803, first published in 1816, and republished in *Gedichte*, Vol. 2, pp. 33-35. According to Klussmann, it represents "eine programmatische Poetik der Lyrik Tiecks."

161. Körner, Josef. "Geheimnis um Ludwig Tieck." *Der kleine Bund*, Berne, 30 October 1938, pp. 353-354; and 6 November 1938, pp. 365-368.

Reveals that Tieck's 1803 sonnets to "Alma" (*Gedichte*, Vol. 1, pp. 185-216) as well as his "Alma" letter were secretly intended for his longtime mistress Henriette von Finckenstein.

162. Loquai, Franz. "Lovells Leiden und die Poesie der Melancholie: Zu Ludwig Tiecks Gedicht *Melankolie*." Pp. 100-113 in *Gedichte und Interpretationen*, Vol. 3: *Klassik und Romantik*, ed. Wulf Segebrecht. Reclams

Universal-Bibliothek, Vol. 7892. Stuttgart: Philipp Reclam jun., 1984. 464 pp.

This *William Lovell* verse insertion, which mirrors the protagonist's penchant for self-reflection, is included in *Gedichte*, Vol. 2, pp. 227-229.

163. Manacorda, Guido. "I 'Reisegedichte' e l'arte di Ludovico Tieck." *Rivista mensile di letteratura tedesca*, 1 (1907): 162-177.

    Analyzes the impressionistic style, atmosphere, and philosophical content of the *Reisegedichte* cycle (1805), which appears in *Gedichte*, Vol. 3, pp. 98-235. See also nos. 167, 168, and 707.

164. Mittner, Ladislao. "Galatea: Die Romantisierung der italienischen Renaissancekunst und -dichtung in der deutschen Frühromantik." *DVLG*, 27 (1953): 555-581.

    Wackenroder's replacement of the heathen Galatea by Madonna in his "Raffaels Erscheinung" and Tieck's subsequent application of the Italian octavo in his 1798 poem "Der Traum" (dedicated to Wackenroder) mark the true beginning of German Romanticism. "Der Traum" can be found in *Gedichte*, Vol. 2, pp. 77-90.

165. Naumann, Walter. *Traum und Tradition in der deutschen Lyrik*. Sprache und Literatur, Vol. 32. Stuttgart, Berlin, Cologne, Mainz: W. Kohlhammer, 1966. 181 pp.

    Contains, on pp. 136-141, an interpretation of Tieck's sonnet "O Wald, was sagst du...?" (1803), published in *Gedichte*, Vol. 3, p. 31.

166. Reitmeyer, Elisabeth. *Studien zum Problem der Gedichtsammlung mit eingehender Untersuchung der Gedichtsammlungen Goethes und Tiecks*. Sprache und Dichtung, Vol. 57. Berne, Leipzig: Paul Haupt, 1935. 258 pp.

As far as Tieck is concerned, Reitmeyer demonstrates (on pp. 121-189) that the *Gedichte* collection is not arranged according to themes or forms, but rather to the inherent musicality of individual poems.

167. Sartori, Gemma. "Spunti per un Ludwig Tieck 'realista': I *Reisegedichte eines Kranken.*" *Annali: Instituto Universitario di Lingue Moderne*, 4 (1975/76): 229-248.

   Interprets several poems of the cycle with an eye on the realistic tendency therein. Also provides details on the background, editorial history, and reception of the cycle, which is printed in *Gedichte*, Vol. 3, pp. 98-235. See also nos. 163, 707, and next item.

168. Stopp, E.C. "The Place of Italy in the Life and Works of Ludwig Tieck." Diss. Cambridge, 1937.

   Of special interest is Stopp's discussion of the *Reisegedichte* (*Gedichte*, Vol. 3, pp. 98-235), in which Italy figures prominently. For more on this cycle, consult nos. 163, 167, and 707. No. 414 contains information on the role of Italy in *Lovell*.

Cross ref.: 666, 672, 690.

### 3. OTHER POEMS

169. Klee, Gotthold. "Kleinigkeiten zu Tiecks Schriften." *Zeitschrift für den deutschen Unterricht*, 9 (1895): 65-67.

   Clarification of problems surrounding Tieck's poetry and literary remains. Includes a previously unpublished occasional poem by Tieck dated 1837.

170. Matenko, Percy. "An Unpublished Ludwig Tieck Poem." *GR*, 5 (1930): 180-182.

A poem dedicating a copy of *Minnelieder aus dem Schwäbischen Zeitalter* (1803) to Graf Friedrich Ludwig Karl von Finckenstein.

171. Zeydel, Edwin H. "A Poem from Tieck to Oehlenschläger." *MLN*, 44 (1929): 179-181.

Addresses some misunderstandings concerning a dedicatory poem dated 1831.

# V. Criticism: Drama

## 1. GENERAL

172. Härtl, Heinz. "Tieck und Lessing." Pp. 526-538 in *Lessing-Konferenz Halle 1979*, Part 2, ed. Hans-Georg Werner. Martin-Luther-Universität Halle-Wittenberg wissenschaftliche Beiträge 1980, Vol. 3 (F 21). Halle (Saale): Martin-Luther-Universität Halle-Wittenberg, 1980. 719 pp.

To a large extent, Tieck followed in Lessing's footsteps when he attempted to create a German national theater, but selected different models and sources for his works, namely Shakespeare and the old German chapbooks.

173. Kaiser, Oscar. *Der Dualismus Ludwig Tiecks als Dramatiker und Dramaturg*. Leipzig: Sturm und Koppe, 1885. 67 pp.

A poorly organized and largely outdated examination.

174. Kluckhohn, Paul. "Die Dramatiker der deutschen Romantik als Shakespeare-Jünger: Festvortrag vor der Hauptversammlung der Deutschen Shakespeare-Gesellschaft 1938." *JDSh*, 74 (1938): 31-49.

Concerning Tieck's dramatic output, argues that Shakespeare's influence led to "Regellosigkeit" and a "zerfließende Mischform."

175. Ulshöfer, Robert. *Die Theorie des Dramas in der deutschen Romantik*. Neue Deutsche Forschungen, Vol. 29. Berlin: Junker und Dünnhaupt, 1935. 183 pp.

Includes commentary on the development of Tieck's dramatic theory, its sources, and its practical manifestation in the form of specific works. Also traces the influence of the philosopher K.W.F. Solger on Tieck's creation of a "symbolisches Drama." Concerning Solger, see also nos. 247 and 650.

176. Wendriner, Karl Georg. *Das romantische Drama: Eine Studie über den Einfluß von Goethes Wilhelm Meister auf das Drama der Romantiker*. Berlin: Oesterheld & Co., 1909. 168 pp.

Links all of Tieck's dramas dealing in any way with the theme of fate to Goethe's "Bildungsroman." Additional references to Goethe's influence on Tieck can be found in nos. 110-112, 237, 443, 690, and 691. For more on fate, see no. 128 as well as next item.

Cross ref.: 673.

## 2. EARLY DRAMAS

### a. General

177. Kraft, Herbert. *Das Schicksalsdrama: Interpretation und Kritik einer literarischen Reihe*. Untersuchungen zur deutschen Literaturgeschichte, Vol. 11. Tübingen: Max Niemeyer, 1974. 127 pp.

A broad survey included here because it offers a rare, albeit brief, discussion of *Der Abschied* and *Karl von Berneck*. More on fate can be found in nos. 128 and 176.

178. Stanger, Hermann. "Der Einfluß Ben Jonsons auf Ludwig Tieck: Ein Abschnitt aus Tiecks Leben und Dichten." *Studien zur vergleichenden Litteraturgeschichte*, 1 (1901): 182-227; and 2 (1902): 37-86.

Useful examination of Jonson's influence on Tieck's earliest dramas and of efforts by Tieck to translate Jonson.

**b. *Das Reh* (1790, pub. 1855)**

179. Regener, Edgar Alfred. *Tieck-Studien: Drei Kapitel zum Thema "Der junge Tieck."* Wilmersdorf-Berlin: O. Reimer, [1903]. 121 pp.

Primarily a treatment of *Das Reh*, which Tieck wrote as a schoolboy.

180. Zeydel, Edwin H. "Das Reh – ein Jugendwerk Ludwig Tiecks." *Euphorion*, 29 (1928): 93-108.

Confirms Tieck's authorship of this work.

**c. *Alla-Moddin* (1790-1791, pub. 1798)**

181. Brunner, Horst. *Die poetische Insel: Inseln und Inselvorstellungen in der deutschen Literatur*. Germanistische Abhandlungen, Vol. 21. Stuttgart: J.B. Metzler, 1967. 294 pp.

Includes brief commentary on the role of the island paradise in Tieck's works, especially in *Alla-Moddin*, which is set in the South Seas.

**d. *Der Abschied* (1792, pub. 1798)**

182. Corkhill, A. "An Interpretation of Ludwig Tieck's Play *Der Abschied*." *AUMLA*, 50 (1978): 261-270.

    The protagonists in this piece are not victims of a fatalistic universe, as has been argued, but rather exercise their will freely.

Cross ref.: 177.

**e. *Karl von Berneck* (1793-1795, pub. 1797)**

183. Hock, Stefan. "Zu Ludwig Tiecks Jugendwerken." *GRM*, 5 (1913): 343.

    A note on the English sources of *Karl von Berneck*.

Cross. ref.: 177.

### 3. SATIRICAL DRAMAS

**a. General**

*i*. Sources

184. Brodnitz, Käthe. *Die vier Märchenkomödien von Ludwig Tieck*. Erlangen: Junge & Sohn, 1912. viii + 101 pp.

    Mostly on the various foreign sources for *Der gestiefelte Kater*, *Ritter Blaubart*, *Rothkäppchen*, and *Däumchen*.

185. Hille, Curt. *Die deutsche Komödie unter der Einwirkung des Aristophanes: Ein Beitrag zur vergleichenden Literaturgeschichte*. Breslauer Beiträge

zur Literaturgeschichte, Vol. 12. Leipzig: Quelle & Meyer, 1907. vi + 180 pp.

Touches briefly on Tieck's satirical pieces (more on Aristophanes in no. 188).

186. Marelli, Adriana. "Ludwig Tiecks frühe Märchenspiele und die Gozzische Manier: Eine vergleichende Studie." Diss. Cologne, 1968.

Like Rusack (next item), demonstrates that Tieck's fairy tale dramas were heavily influenced by Gozzi, but gives more detailed examples.

187. Rusack, Hedwig Hoffmann. *Gozzi in Germany: A Survey of the Rise and Decline of the Gozzi Vogue in Germany and Austria. With Especial Reference to the German Romanticists*. Columbia University Germanic Studies. New York: Columbia University Press, 1930. xiii + 195 pp.

Credits Gozzi with having paved the way for Tieck's new "satirical fairy drama" (see also preceding item).

188. Süss, Wilhelm. *Aristophanes und die Nachwelt*. Das Erbe der Alten: Schriften über Wesen und Wirkung der Antike, Vols. 2-3. Leipzig: Dieterich, 1911. ix + 226 pp.

Builds on no. 185.

*ii*. Satirical Dramas and Irony

189. Immerwahr, Raymond M. *The Esthetic Intent of Tieck's Fantastic Comedy*. Washington University Studies, N.S. Vol. 22. St. Louis: Washington University, 1953. ix + 150 pp.

Tieck's intent in writing his satirical dramas was not to showcase Friedrich Schlegel's concept of irony, but rather to "arouse sustained laughter" (compare with no. 193).

190. Nef, Ernst. "Das Aus-der-Rolle-Fallen als Mittel der Illusionszerstörung bei Tieck und Brecht." *ZDP*, 83 (1964): 191-215.

   On the form, function, and ironic significance of role breaks in comedies by Tieck and Brecht.

191. Strohschneider-Kohrs, Ingrid. *Die romantische Ironie in Theorie und Gestaltung.* Hermaea, N.S. Vol. 6. Tübingen, Max Niemeyer, 1960. 446 pp.

   Describes Tieck's concept of irony as "unscharf und in sich widersprüchlich" on the basis of a thorough evaluation of his satirical plays (see also next item).

192. ___. "Zur Poetik der deutschen Romantik II: Die romantische Ironie." Pp. 75-97 in *Die deutsche Romantik: Poetik, Formen und Motive*, ed. Hans Steffen. Kleine Vandenhoeck-Reihe, Vol. 250. Göttingen: Vandenhoeck & Ruprecht, 1967. 288 pp.

   Essentially a condensed version of the preceding item.

193. Szondi, Peter. "Friedrich Schlegel und die romantische Ironie: Mit einem Anhang über Ludwig Tieck." *Euphorion*, 48 (1954): 397-411.

   Contradicts the conclusions reached in no. 189.

Cross ref.: 138, 139, 201, 204, 206, 215.

### *iii.* Other

194. Arntzen, Helmut. *Die ernste Komödie: Das deutsche Lustspiel von Lessing bis Kleist.* Sammlung Dialog. Munich: Nymphenburger Verlagshandlung, 1968. 304 pp.

   Argues, on pp. 125-155, that Tieck's satirical dramas present "die Welt als Schein."

195. Gentges, Ignaz. "Tiecks Märchenbühne (Die Geste als Wort und Gebärde im Drama Ludwig Tiecks)." *Das deutsche Theater*, 1 (1922/23): 144-160.

This article, a shortened version of Gentges' 1923 Bonn dissertation, attributes the success of Tieck's comedies to the lifelike optical and accoustical devices they employ.

196. Gillespie, Gerald. "Young Tieck and the Romantic Breakthrough." *Theater Three*, 4 (1988): 31-44.

Tieck's satirical dramas greatly influenced the development of the genre in the nineteenth and even twentieth centuries.

197. Hewett-Thayer, Harvey W. "Tieck's Revision of his Satirical Comedies." *GR*, 12 (1937): 147-164.

A general editorial history.

198. Thalmann, Marianne. "Der Manierismus in Ludwig Tiecks Literaturkomödien." *LJGG*, N.S. 5 (1964): 345-351. Reprinted pp. 185-192 in no. 104.

Mannerism in *Der gestiefelte Kater* and *Die verkehrte Welt*. A supplement to no. 118.

199. ___. *Provokation und Demonstration in der Komödie der Romantik: Mit Grafiken zu den Literaturkomödien von Tieck, Brentano, Schlegel, Grabbe und zum Amphitryon-Stoff*. Berlin: Erich Schmidt, 1974. 119 pp.

Pp. 11-69 represent a detailed and highly informative introduction to Tieck's theory of the comedy as well as to his most important comedic works. The accompanying schematics, however, detract from the overall clarity of Thalmann's presentation.

### b. *Der gestiefelte Kater* (1797)

200. Beckmann, Heinz. "Ludwig Tiecks verspätetes Debut." *Rheinischer Merkur*, 14, No. 17 (1959): 8.

    Concerns modern *Kater* stagings.

201. Beyer, Hans Georg. *Ludwig Tiecks Theatersatire "Der gestiefelte Kater" und ihre Stellung in der Literatur- und Theatergeschichte*. Stuttgart: Author, 1960. 208 pp.

    Contends that the piece cannot be viewed as the archetypal romantic comedy because it does not draw the audience into the process of disillusionment and, furthermore, fails to conform to the romantic (i.e., Schlegelian) concept of irony. For more on irony, see nos. 138, 139, 189-193, 204, 206, and 215.

202. Biesterfeld, Wolfgang. "'Spaziergang auf dem Dach der dramatischen Kunst'. Ludwig Tieck: 'Der gestiefelte Kater.'" Pp. 54-64 in *Deutsche Komödien: Vom Barock bis zur Gegenwart*, ed. Winfried Freund. Uni-Taschenbücher, Vol. 1498. Munich: Wilhelm Fink, 1988. 314 pp.

    A useful introduction to the work's sources, genesis, content, and reception.

203. Immerwahr, Raymond. "Iffland in the Role of Tieck's *Kater*." *MLN*, 70 (1955): 195-196.

    Suggests K.A. Böttiger's *Entwickelung des Ifflandischen Spiels* (1796) as a source for various characters in *Kater*.

204. Kreuzer, Helmut. "Tiecks 'Gestiefelter Kater.'" *DU*, 15, No. 6 (1963): 33-44.

    Via a look at *Kater's* play within the play, adds to the irony discussion in nos. 138, 139, 189-193, 201, 206, and 215.

205. Leppmann, Franz. "Der gestiefelte Kater." Pp. 6-10 in Leppmann, *Kater Murr und seine Sippe: Von der Romantik bis zu V. Scheffel und G. Keller.* Munich: C.H. Beck, 1908. 86 pp.

Superficial notes on sources and reception.

206. Matinian, K.R. "Romanticheskaia ironiia v komedii L. Tika 'Kot v sapogakh.'" *VMU*, No. 3 (1985): 62-68.

General comments on irony in *Kater*. See also nos. 138, 139, 189-193, 201, 204, and 215.

207. Paulsell, Patricia R. "Ludwig Tieck's *Der gestiefelte Kater* and the English Burlesque Drama Tradition." *MGS*, 11 (1985): 143-158.

On the influence of Henry Fielding, Richard Brinsley Sheridan, and the Second Duke of Buckingham.

208. Pestalozzi, Karl. "Tieck: Der gestiefelte Kater." Pp. 110-126, 376-379 in *Die deutsche Komödie: Vom Mittelalter bis zur Gegenwart*, ed. Walter Hinck. Düsseldorf: August Bagel, 1977. 411 pp.

In this general introduction, the work is interpreted as a "Demonstration des Scheiterns der Kommunikation zwischen Dichter und Publikum."

209. Reinhard, Ewald. "Ludwig Tiecks 'Gestiefelter Kater.'" *Eichendorff-Kalender*, 11 (1920): 30-39.

Broad and valueless commentary.

210. Wolf, Jacques. "Les Allusions politiques dans le 'Chat botté' de Ludwig Tieck." *Revue Germanique*, 5 (1909): 158-201.

Deals with references to the French Revolution.

Cross ref.: 132, 184, 198, 693.

### c. *Ritter Blaubart* (1797)

211. Alverdes, Paul. "Skandal um Blaubart." *Die Zeit*, Hamburg, 14 June 1951, p. 4.

    Critiques recent German stagings of the play.

Cross ref.: 184.


### d. *Prinz Zerbino* (1796-1798, pub. 1799)

212. Friedrich, Werner P. *Dante's Fame Abroad 1350-1850: The Influence of Dante Alighieri on the Poets and Scholars of Spain, France, England, Germany, Switzerland and the United States. A Survey of the Present State of Scholarship*. University of North Carolina Studies in Comparative Literature. Rome: Edizioni di Storia e Letteratura, 1950. 583 pp.

    Pp. 458-461 contain a note on Dante's brief appearance in *Prinz Zerbino* and a summary of Tieck's various utterances concerning the great Italian. More detailed information on Tieck and Dante can be found in no. 115.

Cross ref.: 113, 691, 715.


### e. *Die verkehrte Welt* (1798, pub. 1799)

213. Behrmann, Alfred. "Wiederherstellung der Komödie aus dem Theater: Zu Tiecks 'historischem Schauspiel' *Die verkehrte Welt*." *Euphorion*, 79 (1985): 139-181.

    A comprehensive introduction including a plot summary and a discussion of the work's characters, themes, structure, language, and reception.

214. Frerking, Johann. "Zwei Shakespeareparodien in Tiecks 'Verkehrter Welt.'" *Euphorion*, 17 (1910): 355-356.

On two *King Lear* parodies.

215. Galaski, Lisa. "Romantische Ironie in Tiecks 'Verkehrter Welt': Zum Verständnis einer artistischen Theaterkomödie aus der Berliner Frühromantik." *RGer*, 14 (1984): 23-57.

    Discovers three levels of irony within the play. See nos. 138, 139, 189-193, 201, 204, and 206 for more on romantic irony.

Cross ref.: 113, 198.


## 4. DRAMAS BASED ON CHAPBOOKS

**a. General**

> *i.* English and German Sources

216. Hense, C.C. "Deutsche Dichter in ihrem Verhältnis zu Shakespeare." *JDSh*, 5 (1870): 107-147; and 6 (1871): 83-128.

    The second part of this article is devoted almost entirely to Shakespeare's influence on *Genoveva, Octavianus,* and *Fortunat* (see also no. 218).

217. Szafarz, Jolanta. "Die Rezeption mittelalterlicher Volksbuchmotive in Ludwig Tiecks Dramen." Pp. 127-140 in *Mittelalter-Rezeption: Gesammelte Vorträge des Salzburger Symposions "Die Rezeption mittelalterlicher Dichter und ihrer Werke in Literatur, Bildender Kunst und Musik des 19. und 20. Jahrhunderts,"* ed. Jürgen Kühnel, Hans-Dieter Mück, and Ulrich Müller. Göppinger Arbeiten zur Germanistik, Vol. 286. Göppingen: Kümmerle, 1979. 631 pp.

Briefly shows how Tieck melded old German chapbook themes with modern (i.e., romantic) poetological concepts in *Genoveva, Octavianus*, and *Fortunat*. Most valuable are the comments concerning the history and development of the legends underlying the named dramas.

218. Żelak, Dominik. *Tieck und Shakespeare: Ein Beitrag zur Geschichte der Shakespearomanie in Deutschland*. Tarnopol: Podolische Buchdruckerei, 1900. 71 pp.

Basically a rehash of no. 216.

### ii. Spanish Sources

219. Behler, Ernst. "The Reception of Calderón Among the German Romantics." *SIR*, 20 (1981): 437-460.

Expands on Tieck's "creative response" to Calderón in *Genoveva* and *Octavianus*, and suggests that it was Tieck's "greatest merit in terms of romantic Calderonismo" that he instigated A.W. Schlegel to translate the Spanish author's work into German.

220. Bertrand, J.-J. A. *L. Tieck et le théatre espagnol*. Bibliothèque de littérature comparée. Paris: F. Rieder, 1914. 182 pp.

Interesting analysis of the influence exerted upon Tieck's later dramatic oeuvre – especially in the areas of form and style – by Calderón, Lope de Vega, and others. Credits Tieck with having introduced Germany to the Spanish drama.

221. Brüggemann, Werner. *Spanisches Theater und deutsche Romantik*, Vol. 1. Spanische Forschungen der Görresgesellschaft, Series 2, Vol. 8. Münster: Aschendorff, 1964. 275 pp.

The commentary on Tieck (pp. 169ff.) represents little more than a modernized version of the preceding item.

222. Hardy, Swana L. *Goethe, Calderon und die romantische Theorie des Dramas*. Heidelberger Forschungen, Vol. 10. Heidelberg: Carl Winter, 1965. 200 pp.

Contains a few notes on Tieck's reception of Calderón. Points out that Goethe became aware of the Spanish author via *Genoveva*.

223. Kern, Hanspeter. "Ludwig Tiecks Calderonismus." *Spanische Forschungen der Görresgesellschaft*, Series 1: *Gesammelte Aufsätze zur Kulturgeschichte Spaniens*, 23 (1967): 189-356.

The most extensive and thoroughly researched study available on Tieck and Calderón. As far as Tieck's works are concerned, focuses primarily on *Genoveva* and *Octavianus*. See also next item.

224. ___. "Calderon und Tiecks Weltbild." *Spanische Forschungen der Görresgesellschaft*, Series 1: *Gesammelte Aufsätze zur Kulturgeschichte Spaniens*, 24 (1968): 337-396.

A continuation of the preceding item, this time with emphasis on Tieck's world view.

*iii*. Other

225. Dux, Karl. *Der Wechsel zwischen Poesie und Prosa im Drama Ludwig Tiecks*. Gießen: von Münchow'sche Universitätsdruckerei, Otto Kind, 1925. 11 pp. Excerpt of Diss. Gießen, 1925.

Analyzes Tieck's motives for interspersing his verse dramas with prose.

**b. *Leben und Tod der heiligen Genoveva* (1800)**

226. Gorm, Ludwig. "Die Technik der Genovevadramen (Müller, Tieck, Hebbel, Ludwig)." *Euphorion*, 17 (1910): 106-111.

   Examines the dramatic techniques applied by Tieck and others in dealing with the complex relationship between Genoveva and Golo.

227. Ranftl, Johann. *Ludwig Tiecks Genoveva als romantische Dichtung*. Grazer Studien zur deutschen Philologie, Vol. 6. Graz: Styria, 1899. vii + 258 pp.

   Still the best study devoted to the play, providing a comprehensive and well-written introduction to its form, style, religious content, "Naturgefühl," reception, and multitude of sources.

228. Rübsam, Gertraut Mathilde. *Stimmungskunst in Tiecks "Genoveva."* Fulda: Parzeller & Co., 1954. 76 pp.

   Restates the obvious by contending that atmosphere not only figures prominently in *Genoveva*, but in all of romantic literature.

229. Schneider, Albert. *La légende de Geneviève de Brabant dans la littérature allemande (Volksbuch, Müller, Tieck, Hebbel, Ludwig)*. Paris: Les Belles Lettres, [1955]. 198 pp.

   A history of the Genoveva theme in Germany.

Cross ref.: 115, 216-224, 656, 686, 704, 721.

## c. *Kaiser Octavianus* (1804)

230. Bodensohn, Anneliese. *Ludwig Tiecks "Kaiser Oktavian" als romantische Dichtung*. Frankfurter Quellen und Forschungen zur germanistischen und romanistischen Philologie, Vol. 20. Frankfurt am Main: Moritz Diesterweg, 1937. 96 pp. Reprinted Hildesheim: H.A. Gerstenberg, 1973.

Of particular interest are the discussions on romantic longing and comedy within the play.

231. Halter, Ernst. *Kaiser Octavianus: Eine Studie über Tiecks Subjektivität*. Zurich: Juris, 1967. 204 pp.

Arrives at virtually the same conclusions as the next item.

232. Lüdtke, Ernst. *Ludwig Tiecks "Kaiser Octavianus": Ein Beitrag zur romantischen Geistesgeschichte*. Kirchhain N.-L.: Max Schmersow, 1925. 236 pp.

Argues that Tieck intended *Octavianus*, with its wealth of forms, themes, and ideas, to represent the ultimate embodiment of "romantische Universalpoesie" (compare with preceding item). Contains a detailed survey of the Octavianus legend in Germany.

Cross ref.: 110, 216-221, 223, 224, 656.

## d. *Fortunat* (1816)

233. Zusman, V.G. and S.V. Sapozhkov. "Dramaticheskaia skazka L. Tika 'Fortunat' v otsenke Pushkina." *IAN*, 48 (1989): 276-282.

On a Russian translation of *Fortunat* and its relationship to the works of Pushkin.

Cross ref.: 216-218, 220, 221.

# VI. Criticism: Prose Fiction

## 1. GENERAL

234. Arendt, Dieter. *Der 'poetische Nihilismus' in der Romantik: Studien zum Verhältnis von Dichtung und Wirklichkeit in der Frühromantik*. Studien zur deutschen Literatur, Vols. 29-30. Tübingen: Max Niemeyer, 1972. xxi + 566 pp.

    Contains an excellent treatment of the nihilistic tendencies in *William Lovell* and a number of Tieck's earlier tales (see also no. 1).

235. Arnold, Paul Joh. "Tiecks Novellenbegriff." *Euphorion*, 23 (1921): 258-271.

    An important and oft-cited introduction to Tieck's theory of the novella that is complemented by nos. 250 and 254.

236. Churbanova, V.S. "Ranniaia proza Tika i problema geroiia v nemetskom romantizme." *VMU*, No. 1 (1989): 64-70.

    Studies the role of the hero in Tieck's romantic prose.

237. Donner, J.O.E. *Der Einfluß Wilhelm Meisters auf den Roman der Romantiker: Akademische Abhandlung.* Helsinki: J.C. Frenckell & Sohn, 1893. iii + 211 pp.

Pp. 34-73 treat the impact of Goethe's "Bildungsroman" on *Franz Sternbald* and "Der junge Tischlermeister" (see also nos. 243 and 443). Additional information on Goethe's influence on Tieck can be found in nos. 110-112, and 176.

238. Fischer, Jens Malte. "'Selbst die schönste Gegend hat Gespenster': Entwicklung und Konstanz des Phantastischen bei Ludwig Tieck." Pp. 131-149 in *Phantastik in Literatur und Kunst*, ed. Christian W. Thomsen and Jens Malte Fischer. Darmstadt: Wissenschaftliche Buchgesellschaft, 1980. x + 563 pp.

Tieck's lifelong interest in the supernatural, the occult, and the demonic provides an important thematic link between his early and late prose.

239. Garmann, Garburg. *Die Traumlandschaften Ludwig Tiecks: Traumreise und Individuationsprozeß aus romantischer Perspektive.* Wiesbaden: Westdeutscher Verlag, 1989. 323 pp.

Analyzes the dreamscapes contained in a variety of early prose works in terms of themes, symbolic value, and significance vis-à-vis the development of self.

240. Garnier, T.D. *Zur Entwicklungsgeschichte der Novellendichtung Ludwig Tieck's.* Gießen: Emil Roth, 1899. 55 pp.

Attempt at a broad classification scheme for Tieck's novellas.

241. Gillespie, Gerald. "German Romantic Realism in the European Context: Reflections on Tieck's, Kleist's, and Meyer's Treatment of History." Pp. 121-135 in *Fide et amore: A Festschrift for Hugo Bekker on his Sixty-Fifth*

*Birthday*, ed. William C. McDonald and Winder McConnell. Göppinger Arbeiten zur Germanistik, Vol. 526. Göppingen: Kümmerle, 1990. xv + 359 pp.

Argues that Tieck – especially in his prose – melded history with modern psychological and ontological thought and thus, like a number of his romantic contemporaries, provided Germans with a new mechanism to cope with and to comprehend the tensions inherent in their collective past.

242. Gottrau, André. *Die Zeit im Werk des jungen Tieck*. Zurich: Ernst Lang, 1947. 135 pp.

Tieck's early prose (especially *William Lovell*) illustrates the transition from the boredom of rationalism to the fantastic dreamworld of Romanticism within German literature of the 1790's (see also no. 251).

243. Jacobs, Jürgen. *Wilhelm Meister und seine Brüder: Untersuchungen zum deutschen Bildungsroman*. Munich: Wilhelm Fink, 1972. 332 pp.

Includes a useful discussion of *Franz Sternbald* and "Der junge Tischlermeister" as examples for the romantic "Bildungsroman."

244. Klussmann, Paul Gerhard. "Ludwig Tieck." Pp. 130-144 in *Handbuch der deutschen Erzählung*, ed. Karl Konrad Polheim. Düsseldorf: August Bagel, 1981. 653 pp.

A well-written introduction to Tieck's prose drawing heavily on new research.

245. Kreuzer, Ingrid. *Märchenform und individuelle Geschichte: Zu Text- und Handlungsstrukturen in Werken Ludwig Tiecks zwischen 1790 und 1811*. Göttingen: Vandenhoeck & Ruprecht, 1983. 190 pp.

From a structural perspective, this study examines the various "Bildkomplexe" denoting Tieck's world view as it is expressed in a variety of his early tales and novels.

246. Lillyman, William J. *Reality's Dark Dream: The Narrative Fiction of Ludwig Tieck*. Berlin, New York: Walter de Gruyter, 1979. ix + 159 pp.

Lillyman incorporates several of his previously published articles (nos. 314, 334, 391, 439, and 455) into this lively commentary on Tieck's "major achievements" as a writer of prose fiction.

247. Mörtl, Hans. "Ironie und Resignation in den Alterswerken Ludwig Tiecks." *Zeitschrift für die österreichischen Mittelschulen*, 2 (1925): 61-94. Reprinted pp. 128-171 in no. 88.

Influenced by Solger, Tieck wanted to present mankind with an alternative to the moral debasement and corruption of modern society by glorifying a "Leben in Gott" in his later prose. More on Tieck and Solger in nos. 175 and 650.

248. Mühl, Beate. *Romantiktradition und früher Realismus: Zum Verhältnis von Gattungspoetik und literarischer Praxis in der Restaurationsepoche (Tieck-Immermann)*. Europäische Hochschulschriften, Series 1: Deutsche Sprache und Literatur, Vol. 599. Frankfurt am Main, Berne: Peter Lang, 1983. iv + 342 pp.

Tieck and Immermann, although rooted in Romanticism, helped to forge a new realistic literature in Germany because they both adapted their later prose to the social, political, and aesthetic ideals of the Biedermeier period.

249. Paulin, Roger. "'Ohne Vaterland kein Dichter': Bemerkungen über historisches Bewußtsein und Dichtergestalt beim späten Tieck." *LJGG*, N.S. 13 (1972): 125-150.

On the historical and nationalistic concerns addressed by Tieck's later narrative fiction.

250. Rowley, Brian A. "To Define True Novellen...: A Taxonomic Enquiry." *PEGS*, N.S. 47 (1977): 4-27.

This attempt at characterizing the German novella deals in large measure with Tieck's theory of the "Wendepunkt" (see also nos. 235 and 254).

251. Scheibe, Friedrich Carl. "Aspekte des Zeitproblems in Tiecks frühromantischer Dichtung." *GRM*, 46 (1965): 50-63.

Whereas no. 242 interprets the theme of boredom in *William Lovell* and other early prose works as an outgrowth of Tieck's own experience, Scheibe seeks an explanation for it within the writings themselves.

252. Scherer, Michael. "Ludwig Tiecks erzählerisches Werk." *Blätter für den Deutschunterricht*, 4 (1960): 12-19.

Superficial overview intended for schoolteachers.

253. Schürk, Brigitte. *Die Geister- und Gespenstererscheinungen in den erzählenden Werken Ludwig Tiecks: Untersuchung eines Motivs und seiner Funktion.* Augsburg: W. Blasaditsch, 1970. 256 pp.

A motif study that centers primarily on *William Lovell*, although other works are also considered.

254. Schunicht, Manfred. "Der 'Falke' am 'Wendepunkt': Zu den Novellentheorien Tiecks und Heyses." *GRM*, 41 (1960): 44-65.

Contends that Tieck applied the term "Wendepunkt" only to his own novellas and did not view it as a general criterion for the genre (compare with nos. 235 and 250).

255. Tecchi, Bonaventura. "Ludovico Tieck poeta realista." *Paragone*, 9, No. 108 (1958): 41-52.

   Describes realistic tendencies within Tieck's later prose.

256. Trainer, James. *Ludwig Tieck: From Gothic to Romantic*. Anglica Germanica, Vol. 8. London, The Hague, Paris: Mouton, 1964. 113 pp.

   Referring to "Abdallah" and *Franz Sternbalds Wanderungen*, Trainer demonstrates how Tieck's Romanticism evolved out of his early preoccupation with Gothic trivial literature. Includes an informative chapter on "Gothic as a literary phenomenon in England." See also nos. 278, 279, 423, and 424.

257. Wesollek, Peter. *Ludwig Tieck oder Der Weltumsegler seines Innern: Anmerkungen zur Thematik des Wunderbaren in Tiecks Erzählwerk*. Wiesbaden: Franz Steiner, 1984. 251 pp.

   This excellent monograph, focusing on the fantastic as a unifying theme within Tiecks narrative fiction, represents one of the sharpest attacks ever mounted against unfair Tieck criticism.

## 2. CONTRIBUTIONS TO NICOLAI'S *STRAUßFEDERN* (1795-1798)

258. Amon, Clara. "Die Straußfedergeschichten: Unter besonderer Berücksichtigung der Beiträge Ludwig Tiecks." Diss. Munich, 1942.

   Still the best and most comprehensive source of information on this topic. Deals extensively with the question of authorship.

259. Fink, Gonthier-Louis. "Die Parodie der bürgerlichen Moral in Tiecks *Kaiser Tonelli.*" *Euphorion*, 67 (1973): 287-305.

"Tonelli" attacks modern society for being too prosaic and materialistic (see also no. 261).

260. Gish, Theodore. "*Vorspiele auf dem Theater*: Dramatical and Theatrical Elements in Ludwig Tieck's *Straußfedern.*" Pp. 51-58 in *Theatrum Mundi: Essays on German Drama and German Literature Dedicated to Harold Lenz on his Seventieth Birthday, September 11, 1978*, ed. Edward R. Haymes. Houston German Studies. Munich: Wilhelm Fink, 1980. iii + 230 pp.

Sheds light on the dramatic passages and drama criticism in Tieck's *Straußfedern* prose.

261. Littlejohns, Richard. "Tonelli und Tunelli: Zu Ludwig Tiecks Märchenparodie." *Euphorion*, 80 (1986): 201-210.

An anonymous German text entitled *Curieuse und sehr merckwürdige Lebens- und Reisebeschreibung eines auf der Wanderschaft sich befindenden Schneider-Gesellen, namentlich Abraham Tunelli* (1750) is identified as the source for Tieck's "Tonelli" of 1798 (see also no. 259).

262. Maassen, C.G. von. "Ludwig Tiecks Straußfedergeschichten: Der Versuch einer Untersuchung." *Der grundgescheute Antiquarius*, 1 (1920/22): 137-151.

Notes on the sources, style, and content of Tieck's numerous *Straußfedern* contributions.

263. Teich, Gabriel. "Die Anfänge von Ludwig Tiecks Novellistik in den 'Straußfedern.'" Diss. Vienna, 1915.

Supposedly available in a privately printed version, this study traces the roots of Tieck's art of the novella to the prose pieces he wrote for Nicolai.

## 3. TALES BASED ON CHAPBOOKS

### a. General

264. Steiner, Bernhard. *Ludwig Tieck und die Volksbücher.* Berlin: C. Vogt, 1893. 63 pp.

Reports on the German chapbook sources for "Die Heymons Kinder," "Die schöne Magelone," and "Geschichtschronik der Schildbürger."

### b. "Die schöne Magelone" (1797)

265. Scheuer, Helmut. "Ludwig Tiecks 'Die schöne Magelone': Ein Vergleich mit dem Volksbuch." Pp. 473-491 in *Mittelalter-Rezeption II: Gesammelte Vorträge des 2. Salzburger Symposions "Die Rezeption des Mittelalters in Literatur, Bildender Kunst und Musik des 19. und 20. Jahrhunderts,"* ed. Jürgen Kühnel, Hans-Dieter Mück, Ursula Müller, and Ulrich Müller. Göppinger Arbeiten zur Germanistik, Vol. 358. Göppingen: Kümmerle, 1982. ix + 772 pp.

Tieck deviated significantly from Veit Warbeck's *Magelonna* chapbook of 1527, which he used as his primary source.

Cross ref.: 264, 665.

c. "Geschichtschronik der Schildbürger" (1797)

266. Wunderlich, Werner. "Ludwig Tiecks Schildbürgerchronik: Der doppelte Spiegel." Pp. 493-514 in *Mittelalter-Rezeption II: Gesammelte Vorträge des 2. Salzburger Symposions"Die Rezeption des Mittelalters in Literatur, Bildender Kunst und Musik des 19. und 20. Jahrhunderts,"* ed. Jürgen Kühnel, Hans-Dieter Mück, Ursula Müller, and Ulrich Müller. Göppinger Arbeiten zur Germanistik, Vol. 358. Göppingen: Kümmerle, 1982. ix + 772 pp.

A discussion on the sources and content of "Schildbürgerchronik," which parodies German enlightened thought.

Cross ref.: 264.

## 4. FAIRY TALE NOVELLAS

a. General

267. Arntzen, Helmut. "Tiecks Märchenerzählung oder die Ambiguität der romantischen Poesie: Ein Vortrag." *MLN*, 103 (1988): 632-647.

Demonstrates that "Eckbert," "Eckart," and "Runenberg" share an important theme: "Der falsche Umgang mit der Poesie führt in den Wahnsinn."

268. Birrell, Gordon. *The Boundless Present: Space and Time in the Literary Fairy Tales of Novalis and Tieck.* University of North Carolina Studies in the Germanic Languages and Literatures, Vol. 95. Chapel Hill: The University of North Carolina Press, 1979. 160 pp.

A careful analysis of the complex and often interrelated spatial and temporal structures in Tieck's "Eckbert" and "Runenberg" as well as in works by Novalis.

269. Böhme, Hartmut. "Romantische Adoleszenzkrisen: Zur Psychodynamik der Venuskult-Novellen von Tieck, Eichendorff und E.T.A. Hoffmann." *Text und Kontext*, Supplement to Vol. 10 (1981): 133-176.

As far as Tieck is concerned, discusses the tendency of protagonists in "Eckart" and "Runenberg" to escape from the dawning industrial age by fleeing into magical mountain realms. For similar interpretations, see nos. 292 and 293.

270. Crisman, William. "Names, Naming and the Presentation of Language in the Fairytales from Tieck's *Phantasus*." *MGS*, 11 (1985): 127-143.

An onomastic examination of "Eckbert," "Eckart," "Runenberg," "Liebeszauber," "Die Elfen," and "Der Pokal."

271. ___. "The Status of Adult Rationality in Tieck's Fairy Tales." *CollG*, 21 (1988): 111-126.

The allegory of "rationality," read into Tieck's tales by successive generations of critics, is identified as a "common ground" between the many disparate interpretations of these works.

272. Fink, Gonthier-Louis. "Le conte fantastique de Tieck." *RGer*, 4 (1974): 71-94.

Tieck's fairy tales focus in large part on the existential struggles of individuals (mostly artists) caught between reality and their own paradisical world of dreams.

273. Haase, Donald P. "Ludwig Tieck: 1773-1853." Pp. 83-89 in *Supernatural Fiction Writers: Fantasy and Horror*, Vol. 1, ed. E.F. Bleiler. New York: Scribner's, 1985. xix + 519 pp.

Good English-language introduction to Tieck's fairy tales. Ideal for students.

274. Hubbs, V.C. "Tieck's Romantic Fairy Tales and Shakespeare." *SIR*, 8 (1968/69): 229-234.

Tieck's portrayal of the supernatural in his tales was heavily influenced by Shakespeare's dramas.

275. Kimpel, Richard W. "Nature, Quest, and Reality in Tieck's *Der blonde Eckbert* and *Der Runenberg*." *SIR*, 9 (1970): 176-192.

A nature-based interpretation of the named works.

276. Klussmann, Paul Gerhard. "Die Zweideutigkeit des Wirklichen in Ludwig Tiecks Märchennovellen." *ZDP*, 83 (1964): 426-452. Reprinted pp. 352-385 in no. 88.

Centers on the real vs. the unreal, the natural vs. the supernatural, and the conscious vs. the unconscious in Tieck's fairy tales. An informative and well-written article.

277. Mazur, Gertrud S. "Ludwig Tiecks Märchen für Erwachsene: Die magische Landschaft der Romantik." *Proceedings: Pacific Northwest Conference on Foreign Languages*, 30 (1979): 68-70.

The "magische Landschaften" found in the fairy tales are portrayed as Tieck's most valuable contribution to German literature.

278. Müller-Dyes, Klaus. "Der Schauerroman und Ludwig Tieck: Über die dichterische Fiktion im 'Blonden Eckbert' und 'Runenberg'. Ein Beitrag zur Wechselbeziehung von Trivialliteratur und Dichtung." Diss. Göttingen, 1965.

Much like nos. 256, 423, and 424, concludes that Tieck's early prose was clearly influenced by Gothic trivial literature. See also next item.

279. ___. "Wechselerhöhung und Erniedrigung: Zum Romantisierungsprozeß in Tiecks 'Blondem Eckbert' und 'Runenberg.'" *Doitsu Bungaku*, 41 (1968): 95-106.

   An outgrowth of the preceding item.

280. Nobuoka, Yorio. "Das Gebirge im Tieckschen Naturmärchen." *Forschungsberichte zur Germanistik*, 8 (1966): 1-15.

   Discusses the importance of mountains within Tieck's early tales.

281. Peuker, Klaus. "Drei Märchennovellen aus Tiecks Phantasus als Einführung in die Romantik." *Pädagogische Provinz*, 12 (1958): 191-199.

   For schoolteachers.

282. Pongs, Hermann. "Grundlagen der deutschen Novelle des 19. Jahrhunderts." *JFDH*, 1930, pp. 151-231.

   Tieck's fairy tales, along with works by Boccaccio, Cervantes, Goethe, E.T.A. Hoffmann, and Kleist, are viewed as precursors of the modern German novella.

283. Schumacher, Hans. *Narziß an der Quelle. Das romantische Kunstmärchen: Geschichte und Interpretationen*. Schwerpunkte Germanistik. Wiesbaden: Athenaion, 1977. 202 pp.

   Contains excellent short interpretations of "Eckbert," "Eckart," "Runenberg," "Liebeszauber," "Die Elfen," and "Der Pokal." Especially useful for students.

284. Stanguennoc, André. "Ontologie et pathologie du symbole dans trois contes de Ludwig Tieck." *Revue Philosophique*, 174 (1984): 3-26. Reprinted pp. 117-143 in Stanguennoc, *Etudes post-kantiennes: Le rationnel*

*et l'irrationnel dans la pensée post-kantienne.* Lausanne: L'Age d'Homme, 1987. 159 pp.

The tales "Eckbert," "Eckart," and "Runenberg" represent a pathological regression from God, ethics, and the world, and thus stand in complete opposition to the progressivism of Hegel (continued in next item).

285. ___. "Ontologie et pathologie du symbole chez L. Tieck (II): Le conte du Tannenhäuser." *Revue Philosophique,* 175 (1985): 3-13. Reprinted pp. 145-156 in Stanguennoc, *Etudes post-kantiennes: Le rationnel et l'irrationnel dans la pensée post-kantienne.* Lausanne: L'Age d'Homme, 1987. 159 pp.

A continuation of the previous item to include the figure of Tannenhäuser in "Eckart."

286. Stickney-Bailey, Susan. "Tieck's *Märchen* and the Enlightenment: The Influence of Wieland and Musäus." Diss. Massachusetts, 1985. Abstract in *DAI,* 46, No. 12A (1986): 3730-3731.

Influence study focusing on Tieck's use of the ambiguous and marvelous in his fairy tales.

287. Thalmann, Marianne. *Das Märchen und die Moderne: Zum Begriff der Surrealität im Märchen der Romantik.* Urban-Bücher, Vol. 53. Stuttgart: W. Kohlhammer, 1961. 112 pp. Translated by Mary B. Corcoran as *The Romantic Fairy Tale: Seeds of Surrealism.* Ann Arbor: The University of Michigan Press, 1964. vii + 133 pp.

Pp. 35-58 are devoted to a general discussion of Tieck's early tales, with special reference to their relationship to reality, their characterization of the individuation process, and their significance for modern literature.

288. ___. *Zeichensprache der Romantik: Mit 12 Strukturzeichnungen.* Poesie und Wissenschaft, Vol. 4. Heidelberg: Lothar Stiehm, 1967. 115 pp. Translated by Harold A. Basilius as *The Literary Sign Language of German Romanticism.* Detroit: Wayne State University Press, 1972. 152 pp.

Examines the symbolic language employed in fairy tales by Tieck and others with the intent of shedding light on the creative process involved in the production of German romantic literature. The accompanying schematics are of limited value.

289. Todsen, Hermann. *Über die Entwicklung des romantischen Kunstmärchens: Mit besonderer Berücksichtigung von Tieck und E.T.A. Hoffmann.* Berlin: Gustav Schade, 1906. 122 pp.

Works by Tieck and Hoffmann are highlighted in this superficial survey of the German "Kunstmärchen" from Goethe to Storm.

290. Wells, Larry D. "Sacred and Profane: A Spatial Archetype in the Early Tales of Ludwig Tieck." *Monatshefte*, 70 (1978): 29-44.

Applies the theory of sacred and profane spaces as postulated by Ernst Cassirer and Mircea Eliade to Tieck's "Eckbert" and "Runenberg."

291. Wührl, Paul-Wolfgang. *Das deutsche Kunstmärchen: Geschichte, Botschaft und Erzählstrukturen.* Uni-Taschenbücher, Vol. 1341. Heidelberg: Quelle & Meyer, 1984. 370 pp.

Significant in that chapter five – "Dämonismus in Tiecks Manier: Das Wunderbare als feindliches Prinzip des Nachtstücks" (pp. 238-282) – places "Eckbert" and "Runenberg" at the beginning of a tradition of German demonic tales extending from E.T.A. Hoffmann, Eichendorff, Arnim, and Storm to Hofmannsthal, Kafka, Werfel, and Dürrenmatt.

Cross ref.: 234, 235, 240, 245, 250, 254, 402, 696.

**b. "Der blonde Eckbert" (1797)**

292. Bürger, Christa. "Der blonde Eckbert: Tiecks romantischer Antikapitalismus." Pp. 139-158 in *Literatursoziologie*, Vol. 2: *Beiträge zur Praxis*, ed. Joachim Bark. Stuttgart, Berlin, Cologne, Mainz: W. Kohlhammer, 1974. 195 pp.

"Eckbert" is symptomatic of the romantic generation's escape into a precapitalistic world of art and idealism and thus also of its inability to cope with social and political change. See also next item and no. 269.

293. ___. "Romantische Gesellschaftskritik: Tiecks Blonder Eckbert." Pp. 9-35 in *Von der romantischen Gesellschaftskritik zur Bejahung des Imperialismus: Tieck, Keller, Kipling*. Literatur und Geschichte: Modellanalysen. Frankfurt am Main, Berlin, Munich: Moritz Diesterweg, 1974. 116 pp.

Similar to the preceding item (compare also with no. 269).

294. Davies, J.M.Q. "*Eckbert the Fair* as Paradigm." *AUMLA*, 73 (1990): 181-189.

First printed in vol. 72 of *AUMLA* with a page missing, this article explores several methodological and critical approaches to the interpretation of "Eckbert" in the context of an undergraduate literary theory seminar.

295. Ellis, John M. "Tieck: 'Der blonde Eckbert.'" Pp. 77-93 in Ellis, *Narration in the German Novelle: Theory and Interpretation*. Anglica Germanica Series 2. Cambridge: Cambridge University Press, 1974. viii + 219 pp.

Shows how "Eckbert" conforms to and illuminates the "possibilities" of the narrative convention of the German fairy tale.

296. Ewton, Ralph W., Jr. "Childhood Without End: Tieck's *Der blonde Eckbert.*" *GQ*, 46 (1973): 410-427.

The mechanisms displayed by Eckbert and Bertha to cope with reality are childish in nature and are based on "hidden motives."

297. Fickert, Kurt J. "The Relevance of the Incest Motif in 'Der blonde Eckbert.'" *GN*, 13 (1982): 33-35.

Much like Lillyman (no. 314), Fickert finds the controversial ending of "Eckbert," in which the incestuous relationship between brother and sister is revealed, to be important for a general understanding of the work. For more on the incest motif, see nos. 136, 137, and 298.

298. Finney, Gail. "Self-Reflexive Siblings: Incest as Narcissism in Tieck, Wagner, and Thomas Mann." *GQ*, 56 (1983): 243-256.

As far as "Eckbert" is concerned, adds to the discussion in nos. 297 and 314 by placing the incest motif into the context of narcissism (consult also nos. 136 and 137). Narcissism, from the perspective of Tieck's biography, is addressed in no. 318.

299. Freund, Winfried. *Literarische Phantastik: Die phantastische Novelle von Tieck bis Storm*. Sprache und Literatur, Vol. 129. Stuttgart, Berlin, Cologne: W. Kohlhammer, 1990. 156 pp.

Includes, on pp. 16-26, an interpretation of "Eckbert" revolving around "das Grauen vor der Leere," itself viewed as a product of the "rationalistische Verengung des 18. Jahrhunderts."

300. Fries, Thomas. "Ein romantisches Märchen: *Der blonde Eckbert* von Ludwig Tieck." *MLN*, 88 (1973): 1180-1211.

An unfocused analysis too often recapitulating the findings of others. Describes "Eckbert" as an "Anti-Märchen," in which the subject, the "Ich," is unconsciously motivated.

301. Gellinek, Janis Little. "*Der blonde Eckbert*: A Tieckian Fall from Paradise." Pp. 147-166 in *Lebendige Form: Interpretationen zur deutschen Literatur. Festschrift für Heinrich E.K. Henel*, ed. Jeffrey L. Sammons and Ernst Schürer. Munich: Wilhelm Fink, 1970. 299 pp.

"Eckbert" is a "subtle allegory of good and evil," in which the fall from the Garden of Paradise is precipitated by Eckbert/Bertha's sin against the magical realm of "Waldeinsamkeit."

302. Greiner, Bernhard. "Patho-logie des Erzählens: Tiecks Entwurf der Dichtung im 'Blonden Eckbert.'" *DU*, 39, No. 1 (1987): 111-123.

The ambiguity in "Eckbert" is attributed to the "personale Erzählweise" and to "wiederholte Verschiebungen zwischen erzählter Welt und Erzählen" (compare with nos. 308, 315, and 319-321).

303. Haenicke, Diether H. "Ludwig Tieck und 'Der blonde Eckbert.'" Pp. 170-187 in *Vergleichen und Verändern: Festschrift für Helmut Motekat*, ed. Albrecht Goetze and Günther Pflaum. Munich: Max Hueber, 1970. 403 pp.

Identifies two levels of reality in "Eckbert," namely "das Gewöhnliche" and "das Wunderbare," the blurring of which ultimately leads to insanity and death.

304. Haeuptner, Gerhard. "Ludwig Tiecks Märchen 'Der blonde Eckbert.'" Pp. 22-26 in *Verstehen und Vertrauen: Otto Friedrich Bollnow zum 65. Geburtstag*, ed. Jo-

hannes Schwartländer. Stuttgart, Berlin, Cologne, Mainz: W. Kohlhammer, 1968. 301 pp.

On historical time (life in the normal world) vs. eternity (life in the realm of "Waldeinsamkeit") in "Eckbert." It is the ill-fated goal of the protagonists to unify these disparate temporal elements.

305. Hahn, Walther L. "Tiecks *Blonder Eckbert* als Gestaltung romantischer Theorie." *Proceedings: Pacific Northwest Conference on Foreign Languages*, 18 (1967): 69-78.

Views "Eckbert" as a testbed for the emerging romantic theory of literature propagated largely by Friedrich Schlegel.

306. Hasselbach, Karlheinz. "Ludwig Tiecks *Der blonde Eckbert*: Ansichten zu seiner historischen Bewertung." *Neophilologus*, 71 (1987): 90-101.

"Eckbert" combines elements of the fairy tale ("Waldeinsamkeit"), the idyll (Eckbert and Bertha's quiet home life), and the fate tragedy (retribution for sins committed).

307. Heinisch, Klaus J. *Deutsche Romantik: Interpretationen.* Wort, Werk, Gestalt. Paderborn: Ferdinand Schöningh, 1966. 220 pp.

Pp. 123-133 contain an interpretation of "Eckbert" showing how Tieck made Germans aware of the human subconscious via this work.

308. Horton, David. "'Verwirrung' in *Der blonde Eckbert.*" *GL&L*, N.S. 37 (1984): 322-335.

Agrees with Swales (no. 320) that the disorientation and mystification of the reader caused by "Eckbert" was calculated on Tieck's part to preclude the development of one simple, unambiguous interpretation (see also nos. 302, 315, 319, and 321).

309. Hubbs, V.C. "Tieck, Eckbert und das kollektive Unbewußte." *PMLA*, 71 (1956): 686-693.

A Jungian interpretation of the characters in "Eckbert" as mythological archetypes.

310. Immerwahr, Raymond. "'Der blonde Eckbert' as a Poetic Confession." *GQ*, 34 (1961): 103-117.

Describes "Eckbert" as a particularly "authentic" piece because it reveals many of its author's "abnormal tendencies."

311. ___. "The Outer World in *Der blonde Eckbert*." Pp. 52-70 in *Studies in Nineteenth Century and Early Twentieth Century German Literature: Essays in Honor of Paul Whitaker*, ed. Norman H. Binger and A. Wayne Wonderley. Germanistische Forschungsketten, Vol. 3. Lexington: APRA Press, 1974. vii + 186 pp.

The outer world, as seen through the eyes of Eckbert and Bertha, is "the backdrop for a drama of irreparable human frailty, of hopelessness and despair, affording happiness only in the transitory stage of childhood innocence."

312. Kauf, Robert. "Interpretation und 'Relevanz': Am Beispiel von *Ritter Gluck, Bergkristall*, und *Der blonde Eckbert*." *UP*, 5 (1972): 56-65.

A collection of interpretations for the classroom.

313. Liedke, Otto K. "Tiecks *Der blonde Eckbert*: Das Märchen von Verarmung und Untergang." *GQ*, 44 (1971): 311-316.

In contrast to the traditional "Volksmärchen," the romantic "Kunstmärchen," as epitomized by "Eckbert," always ends in utter chaos.

314. Lillyman, W. J. "The Enigma of *Der blonde Eckbert*: The Significance of the End." *Seminar*, 7 (1971): 144-155. Revised version pp. 79-92 in no. 246.

The ending of "Eckbert," often considered to be dispensable due to its seemingly unmotivated revelation of incest, is indeed an integral part of the tale necessary for an overall understanding of its meaning and significance. Fickert (no. 297) reaches a similar conclusion. See also nos. 136, 137, and 298.

315. Northcott, Kenneth J. "A Note on the Levels of Reality in Tieck's *Der blonde Eckbert*." *GL&L*, N.S. 6 (1952/53): 292-294.

Five levels of reality are employed in "Eckbert" to establish what Northcott terms "an atmosphere of confusion, bewilderment and tragedy" (compare with nos. 302, 308, and 319-321).

316. Rippere, Victoria L. "Ludwig Tieck's 'Der blonde Eckbert': A Psychological Reading." *PMLA*, 85 (1970): 473-486.

A close reading of "Eckbert" designed to elucidate the "symbolic language" of the text with the help of Freudian terminology.

317. Schlaffer, Heinz. "Roman und Märchen: Ein formtheoretischer Versuch über Tiecks 'Blonden Eckbert.'" Pp. 224-241 in *Gestaltungsgeschichte und Gesellschaftsgeschichte: Literatur-, kunst- und musikwissenschaftliche Studien*, ed. Helmut Kreuzer. Stuttgart: J.B. Metzler, 1969. xii + 624 pp. Reprinted pp. 444-464 in no. 88; and pp. 251-264 in *Romantikforschung seit 1945*, ed. Klaus Peter. Neue Wissenschaftliche Bibliothek, Vol. 93. Königstein/Ts.: Verlagsgruppe Athenäum, Hain, Scriptor, Hanstein, 1980. 380 pp.

"Eckbert" represents a combination of fairy tale form and novelistic content. As such, it is a precursor of the nineteenth century German novella.

318. Sellner, Timothy F. "Jungian Psychology and the Romantic Fairy Tale: A New Look at Tieck's 'Der blonde Eckbert.'" *GR*, 55 (1980): 89-97.

Interprets "Eckbert" as a "prophetic dream," in which the psyche, drawing on the collective and personal unconscious, vicariously acts out a problem – in this case Tieck's narcissistic attachment to his sister Sophie – and arrives at a solution (complements no. 298).

319. Smith, Charlotte K. "Sprachliche Ambivalenz in Ludwig Tiecks *Der blonde Eckbert*." *Proceedings: Pacific Northwest Conference on Foreign Languages*, 30 (1979): 75-78.

Tieck obscured the meaning of "Eckbert" through his frequent use of the subjunctive and of verbs expressing doubt. Contributes to the discussion in nos. 302, 308, 315, 320, and 321.

320. Swales, Martin. "Reading One's Life: An Analysis of Tieck's *Der blonde Eckbert*." *GL&L*, N.S. 29 (1975): 165-175.

Because it functions on disparate levels of reality, the narrative in "Eckbert" invokes "a tension of expectations" leading to interpretive uncertainty on the part of the reader (see also nos. 302, 308, 315, 319, and 321).

321. Tatar, Maria. "Unholy Alliances: Narrative Ambiguity in Tieck's 'Der blonde Eckbert.'" *MLN*, 102 (1987): 608-626.

Ambiguity arises in "Eckbert" via the fusing of two discrete narrative modes, namely that of Eckbert and that of Bertha. For more on the ambiguity question, consult nos. 302, 308, 315, and the preceding two items.

322. Vitt-Maucher, Gisela. "Eckbert, der gescheiterte Romantiker? Eine Strukturanalyse von Tiecks *Der blonde Eckbert.*" Pp. 332-346 in *Wege der Worte: Festschrift für Wolfgang Fleischhauer. Anläßlich seines 65. Geburtstages und des 40. Jahres seines Wirkens als Professor der deutschen Philologie an der Ohio State University mit Beiträgen von Freunden, Kollegen und Schülern*, ed. Donald C. Riechel. Cologne, Vienna: Böhlau, 1978. xvii + 401 pp.

Eckbert exemplifies those German romantics who were unable to attain a harmonious existence.

323. Weigand, Karlheinz. "Zu Tiecks 'Der blonde Eckbert' anhand der Deutung durch Ernst Bloch." *Bloch-Almanach*, 3 (1983): 115-122.

A brief interpretation revolving around Bloch's commentary on "Eckbert" in his essay "Bilder des Déjà vu" (1962).

Cross ref.: 267, 268, 270, 275, 278, 279, 283, 284, 290, 291, 388, 671, 679, 722.

### c. "Der getreue Eckart und der Tannenhäuser" (1799)

324. Begemann, Christian. "Eros und Gewissen: Literarische Psychologie in Ludwig Tiecks Erzählung *Der getreue Ekkart und der Tannenhäuser.*" *IASL*, 15, No. 2 (1990): 89-145.

Detailed analysis showing how – in terms of its expression of erotic feeling, repressed desires, and inner strife – Tieck's story is still very much a product of the Enlightenment.

325. Hertel, Theodor. *Über Ludwig Tieck's Getreuen Eckart und Tannenhäuser*. Marburg a. L.: Robert Noske, 1917. 96 pp.

A general, but rather uncritical, introduction to "Eckart" focusing on sources, style, language, content, editorial history, and reception.

326. Nollendorfs, Cora Lee. "The Kiss of the Supernatural: Tieck's Treatment of a Familiar Legend." Pp. 154-167 in *Fairy Tales as Ways of Knowing: Essays on Märchen in Psychology, Society and Literature*, ed. Michael M. Metzger and Katharina Mommsen. Germanic Studies in America, Vol. 41. Berne, Frankfurt am Main, Las Vegas: Peter Lang, 1981. 198 pp.

Focuses on the theme of "confusion between the real and the unreal" in "Eckart" and portrays the supernatural elements in this tale as "an unsettling and mystifying invasion [...] on the real world of our everyday lives."

Cross ref.: 267, 269, 270, 283-285.

### d. "Der Runenberg" (1804)

327. Bertrand, J.-J. A. "Le Conte fantastique chez L. Tieck ('Der Runenberg')." *Revue de l'enseignement des langues vivantes*, 43 (1925): 61-65, 109-116.

Interprets "Runenberg" as a depiction of the elemental conflict between man and nature.

328. Diez, Max. "Metapher und Märchengestalt." *PMLA*, 48 (1933): 74-99, 488-507, 877-894, 1203-1222.

Pp. 877-887, devoted to "Runenberg," illustrate how the mountain is transformed into a demon within the demented protagonist's soul.

329. Ewton, Ralph W., Jr. "Life and Death of the Body in Tieck's *Der Runenberg*." *GR*, 50 (1975): 19-33.

Using Jakob Böhme's mystic cosmogony as a basis for his study, Ewton contends that "Runenberg" explores the problem of "affirming life in a body which dies." Additional information on Tieck and Böhme can be found in nos. 107, 330, and 340.

330. Fink, Gonthier-Louis. "Le *Runenberg* de L. Tieck: Fantastique et Symbolisme." *RGer*, 8 (1978): 20-49.

Within the context of a comprehensive analysis of "Runenberg," Fink examines (much like the preceding item) the influence of Böhme on this tale. Concerning Böhme, see also nos. 107 and 340.

331. Frye, Lawrence O. "Irretrievable Time and the Poems in Tieck's 'Der Runenberg.'" *LJGG*, N.S. 18 (1977): 147-171.

Interprets the three verse insertions in this story. Consider also no. 159.

332. Knight, Victor. "The Perceptive Non-Artist: A Study of Tieck's *Der Runenberg*." *NGS*, 10 (1982): 21-31.

Christian, the "perceptive non-artist" in "Runenberg," is "debased" for, though his "vision of beauty is wonderful, its implementation in social reality is a disaster."

333. Kremer, Detlef. "Die Schrift des 'Runenbergs': Literarische Selbstreflexion in Tiecks Märchen." *JJPG*, 24 (1989): 117-144.

On Tieck's penchant for self-reflection in his early tales, particularly in "Runenberg."

334. Lillyman, W.J. "Ludwig Tieck's 'Der Runenberg': The Dimensions of Reality." *Monatshefte*, 62 (1970): 231-244. Revised version pp. 92-107 in no. 246.

The characters in "Runenberg" see the mountain as representing either demonic forces or true divinity. Lillyman argues that the text discourages readers from accepting either view by presenting reality as something that is beyond human definition (see also nos. 336 and 337).

335. Mecklenburg, Norbert. "'Die Gesellschaft der verwilderten Steine': Interpretationsprobleme von Ludwig Tiecks Erzählung 'Der Runenberg.'" *DU*, 34, No. 6 (1982): 62-76.

Warns against an overly rigid interpretation of the tale, as the text was designed by Tieck to promote "Mehrdeutigkeit und Offenheit."

336. Rasch, Wolfdietrich. "Blume und Stein: Zur Deutung von Ludwig Tiecks Erzählung *Der Runenberg*." Pp. 113-128 in *The Discontinuous Tradition: Studies in German Literature in Honour of Ernest Ludwig Stahl*, ed. P.F. Ganz. Oxford: Clarendon Press, 1971. ix + 279 pp.

Contrary to Goethe's views on nature as well as to general expectation, Tieck accords less status to the organic world of the living than to the dead, inorganic realm of stone in "Runenberg" (compare with nos. 334 amd 337).

337. Tatar, Maria M. "Deracination and Alienation in Ludwig Tieck's *Der Runenberg*." *GQ*, 51 (1978): 285-304.

Focuses on the mandrake root, which became the basis for Christian's "transgression against nature." Interprets the shared syllable in "Runenberg" and "Alrunenwurzel" to imply that the respective realms of nature symbolized by these terms, namely the inorganic and the organic, are much more alike than is assumed in nos. 334 and 336.

338. Vredeveld, Harry. "Ludwig Tieck's *Der Runenberg*: An Archetypal Interpretation." *GR*, 49 (1974): 200-214.

A Jungian interpretation concerned with "ambivalent realms."

339. Whitinger, Raleigh. "Novalis' Influence on *Der Runenberg*: On Ludwig Tieck's Contribution to Early Romanticism's Image of the Artist." *CGP*, 17 (1989): 53-65.

While it "pays homage to Novalis' idealistic visions of the artist as saviour and mediator of lost wonders," "Runenberg" also "addresses itself to the complexities of modern existence and of human nature that thwart that ideal – thus anticipating later, more 'realistic' trends."

Cross ref.: 267-270, 275, 278, 279, 283, 284, 290, 291, 388, 700.

### e. "Liebeszauber" (1812)

340. Richer, Jean. "Les sept principes dans 'Amour et Magie' de Ludwig Tieck." *Liberté*, 87/88 (1973): 146-161.

Identifies each of the characters in "Liebeszauber" with one of the seven principles outlined in Böhme's mysticism. For more on Tieck and Böhme, see nos. 107, 329, and 330.

Cross ref.: 270, 283.

### f. "Die Elfen" (1812)

341. Favier, Georges. "L'age de raison. Note sur un conte de Tieck: *Die Elfen*." Pp. 47-91 in *Études allemandes: Recueil dédié à Jean-Jacques Anstett*, ed. Georges Brunet. Lyon: Presses Universitaires de Lyon, 1979. vii + 276 pp.

A general introduction to "Die Elfen" portaying this tale as an attack against the Age of Enlightenment.

Cross ref.: 270, 283.

## 5. LATER NOVELLAS

a. General

### i. Later Novellas and Young Germany

342. Bauer, Frieda. "Ludwig Tieck und das junge Deutschland." Diss. Vienna, 1952.

This superficial study of the novellas directed against Young Germany is little more than a rehash of no. 345.

343. Bloesch, Hans. *Das Junge Deutschland in seinen Beziehungen zu Frankreich*. Untersuchungen zur neueren Sprach- und Literaturgeschichte, Vol. 1. Berne: Francke, 1903. 136 pp.

Pp. 81-86 present an overview of Tieck's "Antijungdeutsche Novellen."

344. Hasiński, Maksymilian. *Tiecks Verhältnis zum jungen Deutschland*. Breslau: H. Fleischmann, 1920. 3 pp. Excerpt of Diss. Breslau, 1920.

Limited only to the title page and the author's vita, this excerpt is all that remains of the dissertation which, according to Polish library sources, was lost during World War II.

345. Kiel, Hanna. *Ludwig Tieck und das junge Deutschland*. [Germany]: n.p., n.d. 4 pp. Excerpt of Diss. Munich, 1922.

Kiel's dissertation represents the most informative and critical commentary available on Tieck's novellas directed against the Young Germans.

346. Knudsen, Hans. "Das junge Deutschland' und die Romantik." *Euphorion*, 24 (1922): 423-424.

Excerpt of a previously unpublished letter from Theodor Mundt to Heinrich Koenig dated 5 February 1836, in which Mundt (a member of Young Germany) justifies his vehement rejection of Tieck's later novellas.

347. Laube, Heinrich. "Ludwig Tieck." Pp. 145-169 in Laube, *Moderne Charakteristiken*, Vol. 2. Mannheim: C. Löwenthal, 1835. 428 pp.

Essentially a negative reaction to Tieck's "antijungdeutsche Novellen" by one of the individuals directly attacked. Criticizes Tieck for allegedly having trivialized important German social and political matters in his later novellas.

Cross ref.: 134, 351, 352, 367.

*ii.* Other

348. Conen, Franz. *Die Form der historischen Novelle bei Ludwig Tieck*. M. Gladbach: B. Kühlen, 1914. 45 pp.

The complex of themes and problems treated by Tieck in his later novellas remained remarkably constant.

349. Endrulat, Helmut. "Ludwig Tiecks Altersnovellistik und das Problem der ästhetischen Subjektivität." Diss. Münster, 1957.

Man's search for "eine ästhetische Existenz" in the face of often very trying historical and social circumstances is a unifying theme within the body of Tieck's later novellas.

350. Ewald, Karl. *Die deutsche Novelle im ersten Drittel des neunzehnten Jahrhunderts*. Göttingen: Friedrich Haensch, 1907. 68 pp.

Pp. 50-63, devoted to Tieck, show that his later novellas are characterized by didactic goals on the one hand, and by a style of presentation rooted in dialogue on the other.

351. Fischer, Elfriede. "Zeiteinflüsse auf Tiecks Novellen." Diss. Vienna, 1948.

   Discussion of current events influencing Tieck's "Altersnovellen" (see also no. 367).

352. Gneuss, Christian. *Der späte Tieck als Zeitkritiker*. Literatur in der Gesellschaft, Vol. 4. Düsseldorf: Bertelsmann, 1971. 164 pp.

   A careful, insightful analysis of the criticism found in Tieck's later novellas vis-à-vis Goethe, Romanticism, Biedermeier, and Young Germany. Supersedes no. 134.

353. Heinichen, Jürgen. "Das späte Novellenwerk Ludwig Tiecks: Eine Untersuchung seiner Erzählweise." Diss. Heidelberg, 1963.

   Describes Tieck's "Altersnovellen" as "gesellschaftsnah" in terms of content and style, but indicates that they are not to be viewed as "geschlossene formale Gebilde" because of persistent stylistic and structural inadequacies.

354. Hienger, Jörg. "Romantik und Realismus im Spätwerk Ludwig Tiecks." Diss. Cologne, 1955.

   In contrast to no. 97, argues for the coexistence of both romantic and realistic elements not only in Tieck's later novellas, but in his entire oeuvre – a view shared by many later critics (see, for example, nos. 149 and 150).

355. Hummer, Margarethe. "Ludwig Tieck: Die Frauengestalten in den Dresdner Novellen." Diss. Vienna, 1947.

   With the exception of no. 144, the only study dealing with the role of women in Tieck's works, here in his later novellas. Needs to be revised and brought into line with modern feminist theory.

356. Kimmerich, Peter. *Ludwig Tieck als Novellendichter in seiner entwicklungsgeschichtlichen Bedeutung.* Bonn: Rhenania-Druckerei, 1921. 14 pp. Excerpt of Diss. Bonn, 1921.

Although Kimmerich contends that Tieck's later novellas provided an important catalyst for the development of a realistic literature in Germany, he downgrades them as works of art on the basis of their purported unoriginality and lack of resonance among readers.

357. Klein, Johannes. "Ludwig Tieck." Pp. 163-181 in Klein, *Geschichte der deutschen Novelle von Goethe bis zur Gegenwart*, 4th ed. Wiesbaden: Franz Steiner, 1960. xx + 674 pp.

Included here because it emphasizes a number of Tieck's "Dresdner Novellen" largely overlooked by other critics.

358. Klussmann, Paul Gerhard. "Idylle als Glücksmärchen in Romantik und Biedermeierzeit: Bemerkungen zu Erzählungen und Taschenbuchnovellen Ludwig Tiecks." Pp. 41-59 in *Idylle und Modernisierung der europäischen Literatur des 19. Jahrhunderts*, ed. Hans Ulrich Seeber and Paul Gerhard Klussmann. Abhandlungen zur Kunst-, Musik- und Literaturwissenschaft, Vol. 372. Bonn: Bouvier, 1986. 152 pp.

The idylls employed by Tieck in his later novellas are spiked with satirical elements directed against contemporary society and, hence, can only be described as anti-idylls.

359. Lewy, Käthe. *Die Problemwelt in Ludwig Tiecks Novellen aus den Jahren 1820-1830.* Greifswald: Hans Adler, 1923. 4 pp. Excerpt of Diss. Greifswald, 1923.

Concludes that Tieck's "Altersnovellen" strike a much more optimistic note than his early prose.

360. Minor, Jakob. "Tieck als Novellendichter." *Akademische Blätter*, 1 (1884): 129-161, 193-220. Reprinted pp. 45-127 in no. 88.

An early and important attempt at bolstering Tieck's sagging image by offering a fair appraisal of his "mit Unrecht vergessenen Dichtungen," specifically his "Dresdner Novellen," which – within the context of a general introduction – are divided into six broad categories.

361. Ottmann, Dagmar. *Angrenzende Rede: Ambivalenzbildung und Metonymisierung in Ludwig Tiecks späten Novellen*. Stauffenburg Colloquium, Vol. 17. Tübingen: Stauffenburg, 1990. 187 pp.

Interpretations, from a metonymic perspective, of Tieck's later novellas, including some, which have not previously been subjected to any sort of thorough critical examination.

362. Schaum, Marta. *Das Kunstgespräch in Tiecks Novellen*. Gießener Beiträge zur deutschen Philologie, Vol. 15. Gießen: Otto Kindt, 1925. 84 pp.

Tieck developed the "Novelle mit Kunstgespräch," as exemplified by his later "Dichterleben" and "Tod des Dichters," in order to unify didactic purposes (*prodesse*) with artistic themes (*delectare*).

363. Schläfer, Ute. "Das Gespräch in der Erzählkunst Ludwig Tiecks." Diss. Munich, 1969.

The only study focusing exclusively on the form and function of discussions in Tieck's so-called "Gesprächsnovellen" of the Dresden period.

364. Schröder, Rolf. *Novelle und Novellentheorie in der frühen Biedermeierzeit*. Studien zur deutschen Literatur, Vol. 20. Tübingen: Max Niemeyer, 1970. 243 pp.

Should Tieck's later "Großnovellen" more adequately be termed novels? Schröder addresses himself to this question on pp. 20-52.

365. Stamm, Ralf. *Ludwig Tiecks späte Novellen: Grundlage und Technik des Wunderbaren*. Studien zur Poetik und Geschichte der Literatur, Vol. 31. Stuttgart, Berlin, Cologne, Mainz: W. Kohlhammer, 1973. 156 pp.

Utilizing numerous well-chosen examples, illustrates how Tieck's idea of "das Wunderbare im Alltäglichen," first formulated in 1822, became the basis of many of his later novellas.

366. Thalmann, Marianne. *Ludwig Tieck, "Der Heilige von Dresden": Aus der Frühzeit der deutschen Novelle*. Quellen und Forschungen zur Sprach- und Kulturgeschichte der germanischen Völker, N.S. Vol. 3. Berlin: Walter de Gruyter, 1960. vi + 194 pp.

Attempts to draw scholarly attention to Tieck's "Altersnovellen" by subjecting them to a new and rather elaborate classification scheme based on "die Jahresringe der Produktion" and on "der Entwicklungsablauf dieses Schrifttums."

367. Wiens, Abram G. "Tieck's 'Novellen' from 1821 to 1840 as a Mirror of the Times." Diss. Ohio State, 1935.

A precursor to no. 351.

368. Zeydel, Edwin H. "Ludwig Tieck und das Biedermeier." *GRM*, 26 (1938): 352-358.

With reference to content and style, associates Tieck's novellas from the period 1820-1840 with the term "Biedermeier."

Cross ref.: 6, 235, 240, 250, 254, 429, 650.

### b. "Die Gemälde" (1822)

369. [Sanders, Daniel]. "Aus Tieck's Novelle: Die Gemälde." *Zeitschrift für deutsche Sprache*, 2 (1888): 17-24, 77-86, 112-120.

   Excerpts of the novella are commented upon in terms of content and especially grammar.

### c. "Der Geheimnisvolle" (1823)

370. [Sanders, Daniel]. "Zu L. Tieck's Novelle 'Der Geheimnisvolle' (Dresden 1823)." *Zeitschrift für deutsche Sprache*, 3 (1890): 273-277.

   A grammatical analysis.

### d. "Die Reisenden" (1824)

371. Nobuoka, Yorio. "L. Tiecks Novelle 'Die Reisenden': Ein Beitrag zu seiner späteren Dichtung." *Forschungsberichte zur Germanistik*, 7 (1965): 13-32.

   This novella is characteristic of Tieck's "schwankender Novellenbegriff" because it continually oscillates between the romantic and the realistic.

### e. "Musikalische Leiden und Freuden" (1824)

372. Schoolfield, George C. *The Figure of the Musician in German Literature*. University of North Carolina Studies in the Germanic Languages and Literatures, Vol. 19. Chapel Hill: The University of North Carolina Press, 1956. xv + 204 pp.

Pp. 30-31, 36-37, 44-46, and 58-59 include information concerning the musician characters in "Musikalische Leiden und Freuden."

### f. "Dichterleben" (1826-1831)

373. Eichler, Albert. "Zur Quellengeschichte und Technik von L. Tiecks Shakespeare-Novellen." *Englische Studien*, 56 (1922): 254-280.

    A general introduction to the sources, content, and structure of the "Dichterleben" cycle of novellas.

374. Hecker, Max, "Shakespeares Bild im Spiegel deutscher Dichtung: Vortrag, gehalten am 3. Oktober 1932 vor der Deutschen Shakespeare-Gesellschaft." *JDSh*, 68 (1932): 36-55.

    Includes a note on Tieck's portrayal of Shakespeare in "Dichterleben."

375. Ludwig, Albert. "Shakespeare als Held deutscher Dramen." *JDSh*, 54 (1918): 1-21.

    Credits "Dichterleben" with having presented the first truly accurate picture of Shakespeare's life – a picture which then heavily influenced the many nineteenth century German dramas centering on Shakespeare.

Cross ref.: 362, 576.

### g. "Der funfzehnte November" (1827)

376. Klett, Dwight A. "'Eine schwere Heimsuchung': Nature as an Avenging Force in Ludwig Tieck's 'Der funfzehnte November.'" *West Virginia University Philological Papers*, 37 (1991): 32-38.

Interprets the novella as a work of social criticism, in which nature punishes mankind for its hypocrisy, inhumanity, and godlessness.

Cross ref.: 717, 719.

### h. "Der Alte vom Berge" (1828)

377. Müller, Joachim. "Tiecks Novelle 'Der Alte vom Berge': Ein Beitrag zum Problem der Gattung." *Wissenschaftliche Zeitschrift der Friedrich-Schiller-Universität Jena*, 8 (1958/59): 475-481. Reprinted pp. 303-321 in no. 88.

Tieck combines the themes of crime, magic, and the demonic in "Der Alte" to attack money as the primary force behind the evil and inhumane structures of modern industrial capitalism.

### i. "Der Mondsüchtige" (1832)

378. Schmidt, Erich. "Über Shakespeares Grabdenkmal in Stratford." *JDSh*, 44 (1908): 150.

Cites a passage from the novella concerning Shakespeare's headstone.

### j. "Eine Sommerreise" (1834)

379. Matenko, Percy. "Tieck's Diary Fragment of 1803 and his Novelle *Eine Sommerreise*." *JEGP*, 36 (1937): 83-102.

On the similarities between Tieck's 1803 diary entries concerning a summer trip (June 21-July 12) undertaken with his friend Burgsdorff and events in his travel novella. Includes a first transcription of the diary fragment in question.

### k. "Tod des Dichters" (1834)

380. Bertrand, J.-J. A. "Camoëns en Allemagne." *RLC*, 5 (1925): 246-263.

    Tieck's representation of the Portuguese author in his novella deviates considerably from historical fact.

381. Pratas, Maria. "Camões na Alemanha." *Brotéria*, 97 (1973): 476-492.

    A general reception study including information on "Tod des Dichters."

Cross ref.: 362.

### l. "Der Wassermensch" (1835)

382. Heinisch, Klaus J. *Der Wassermensch: Entwicklungsgeschichte eines Sagenmotivs*. Stuttgart: Klett-Cotta, 1981. 357 pp.

    Pp. 298-306 are devoted to a discussion of Tieck's novella.

### m. "Eigensinn und Laune" (1836)

383. McKinstry, Brian Edmund John. "The Question of Tieck's Liberalism: A Study of *Eigensinn und Laune*." Diss. University of California, 1981. Abstract in *DAI*, 42, No. 03A (1981): 1167.

    This well-written dissertation has a twofold purpose, namely to prove that Tieck was, politically speaking, "a dedicated moderate liberal," and to illustrate the "artistic merit" of "Eigensinn und Laune" via an analysis of its "sophisticated" narrative structures.

n. "Der junge Tischlermeister" (1836)

384. Koopmann, Helmut. *Freiheitssonne und Revolutionsgewitter: Reflexe der Französischen Revolution im literarischen Deutschland zwischen 1789 und 1840.* Tübingen: Max Niemeyer, 1989. vii + 231 pp.

As far as Tieck is concerned, argues that the reconciliation between German nobility and bourgeoisie stands in the foreground of "Tischlermeister."

385. Mörtl, Hans. "Dämonie und Theater in der Novelle 'Der junge Tischlermeister': Zum Shakespeare-Erlebnis Ludwig Tiecks." *JDSh*, 66 (1930): 145-159.

The staging of Shakespeare's *As You Like it* in "Tischlermeister" is symbolic of Tieck's vision of an ideal world.

386. Schwering, Markus. *Epochenwandel im spätromantischen Roman: Untersuchungen zu Eichendorff, Tieck und Immermann.* Kölner germanistische Studien, Vol. 19. Cologne, Vienna: Böhlau, 1985. xii + 270 pp.

"Tischlermeister," like Eichendorff's *Ahnung und Gegenwart* and Immermann's *Die Epigonen*, is symptomatic of the transition from Romanticism to Realism in Germany.

Cross ref.: 113, 237, 243, 566.

o. "Des Lebens Überfluß" (1839)

387. Baumgärtner, Alfred Clemens. "Ludwig Tieck: Des Lebens Überfluß." Pp. 125-139 in *Deutsche Novellen von Goethe bis Walser: Interpretationen für den Literaturunterricht*, Vol. 1: *Von Goethe bis C.F. Meyer*, ed. Jakob Lehmann. Scriptor Taschenbücher:

Literatur + Sprache + Didaktik, Vol. 155. Königstein/Ts.: Scriptor, 1980. 326 pp.

A pedagogical approach to the novella focusing largely on the issue of suspense.

388. Belgardt, Raimund. "Poetic Imagination and External Reality in Tieck: From Divergence to Convergence." Pp. 41-61 in *Essays on German Literature in Honour of G. Joyce Hallamore*, ed. Michael S. Batts and Marketa Goetz Stankiewicz. Toronto: University of Toronto Press, 1968. viii + 255 pp.

"Des Lebens Überfluß" resolves the "dualism between the higher talents of man and external reality" forming the basis of Tieck's early tales "Eckbert" and "Runenberg."

389. Gould, Robert. "Tieck's *Des Lebens Überfluß* as a Self-Conscious Text." *Seminar*, 26 (1990): 237-255.

Describes "Des Lebens Überfluß" as a sort of autobiographical work, in which the protagonist, Heinrich, mimics Tieck's own acts of linguistic creation and manipulation.

390. Hahn, Walther L. "Erzähler und Erzählvorgang in Tiecks *Des Lebens Überfluß*." Pp. 37-49 in *Studies in Nineteenth Century and Early Twentieth Century German Literature: Essays in Honor of Paul K. Whitaker*, ed. Norman H. Binger and A. Wayne Wonderley. Germanistische Forschungsketten, Vol. 3. Lexington: APRA Press, 1974. vii + 186 pp.

The narrator's function in this "Gesprächsnovelle" is to mediate between the characters involved in the discussion, with the purpose of upholding the "geistige Haltung und Weltsicht [...] der Restauration."

391. Lillyman, W.J. "Ludwig Tieck's *Des Lebens Überfluß*: The Crisis of a Conservative." *GQ*, 46 (1973): 393-409. Revised version pp. 116-130 in no. 246.

"Des Lebens Überfluß" is a realistic work centering on the here and now. It is thus not a fairy tale and does not aspire to romantic transcendence as alleged in nos. 393-395.

392. Linn, Rolf N. "Ludwig Tiecks Dienerin Christine." *WB*, 18, No. 12 (1972): 164-170.

A Marxist interpretation accusing Tieck of disinterest in the plight of the working class on the basis of his "erbarmungslose Beschreibung" of the servant Christine in "Des Lebens Überfluß."

393. Oesterle, Ingrid. "Ludwig Tieck: *Des Lebens Überfluß* (1838)." Pp. 231-267 in *Romane und Erzählungen zwischen Romantik und Realismus: Neue Interpretationen*, ed. Paul Michael Lützeler. Stuttgart: Philipp Reclam jun., 1983. 463 pp.

According to Oesterle, this novella proves that romantic ideology can continue to exist in a realistic world characterized by blatant materialism (compare with no. 391 as well as with next two items).

394. Rutz, Wilhelm. "Tiecks Novelle *Des Lebens Überfluß* in ihrem Verhältnis zur Romantik." *Pädagogische Warte*, 41 (1934): 207-217.

In contrast to no. 391, proclaims "Des Lebens Überfluß" to be a distinctly romantic work, which places the individual above society and rejects all enlightened thought (see also nos. 393 and 395).

395. Wiese, Benno von. "Ludwig Tieck: Des Lebens Überfluß." Pp. 117-133 in Wiese, *Die deutsche Novelle von Goethe bis Kafka*, Vol. 1. Düsseldorf: August Bagel, 1956. 350 pp.

**Romantic elements are just as prevalent as realistic ones in this work (consult also nos. 391, 393, and 394).**

## 6. NOVELS

### a. General

#### *i.* Sources

396. Brüggemann, Werner. *Cervantes und die Figur des Don Quijote in der Kunstanschauung und Dichtung der deutschen Romantik.* Spanische Forschungen der Görresgesellschaft, Series 2, Vol. 7. Münster: Aschendorff, 1958. 380 pp.

Pp. 147-174 are of special interest as they document the influence of *Don Quixote* on *William Lovell* and *Franz Sternbald* (see also nos. 113 and 114).

397. Hubert, Ulrich. *Karl Philipp Moritz und die Anfänge der Romantik: Tieck, Wackenroder, Jean Paul, Friedrich und August Wilhelm Schlegel.* Frankfurt am Main: Athenäum, 1971. xxiii + 229 pp.

The psychological novel *Anton Reiser* had a profound impact on *Lovell* and *Sternbald*.

398. Nehrkorn, Hans. *Wilhelm Heinse und sein Einfluß auf die Romantik.* Goslar: F.A. Lattmann, 1904. 84 pp.

Pp. 42-67 demonstrate the influence of Heinse's *Ardinghello* on *Lovell, Sternbald,* and *Vittoria Accorombona.*

#### *ii.* Other

399. Bent, M.I. "Pozdniaia novellistika Liudviga Tika: Problema metoda i zhanra." *IAN*, 49 (1990): 372-379.

A general introduction to Tieck's novels, with special emphasis on their development and their conformity to the genre.

400. Blackall, Eric A. *The Novels of the German Romantics*. Ithaca, London: Cornell University Press, 1983. 315 pp.

Contains broad introductions to *Lovell* and *Sternbald* that are geared primarily to students.

401. Ewers, Hans-Heino. "Kindheit zwischen Frömmigkeit und Sentimentalität: Kindheitsmotive im literarischen Frühwerk Ludwig Tiecks." Pp. 203-256 in Ewers, *Kindheit als poetische Daseinsform: Studien zur Entstehung der romantischen Kindheitsutopie im 18. Jahrhundert. Herder, Jean Paul, Novalis und Tieck*. Munich: Wilhelm Fink, 1989. 270 pp.

An examination of the "Metaphysik der Kindheit" in *Lovell* and *Sternbald* constitutes the chapter on Tieck. This "Metaphysik" oscillates between "Wahrheit" and "Schein" and is mediated by irony.

402. Lindig, Horst. *Der Prosastil Ludwig Tiecks*. Leipzig: Schnurpfeil & Steinmetz, 1937. 139 pp.

Based on a close reading of *Lovell, Sternbald, Vittoria Accorombona*, and a number of early tales, concludes that Tieck exhibits a definite inclination toward superlatives, alliteration, antithetical constructions, extreme pathos as well as empty and redundant words and phrases in his prose. Outdated and unfair.

### b. *William Lovell* (1793-1796, pub. 1795-1796)

403. Beckers, Gustav. "Die Darstellung der proteischen Seelen-Existenz Ludwig Tiecks im 'William Lovell.'" Pp. 7-17 in Beckers, *Versuche zur dichterischen Schaffensweise deutscher Romantiker (Ludwig Tieck, Friedrich Schlegel, Clemens Brentano)*. Acta Jutlandica, Vol. 33. Copenhagen: Ejnar Munksgaard, 1961. 48 pp.

*Lovell* is a portrait of Tieck's own "Seelenleben," which is characterized by a fundamental dichotomy between the psychic and the rational.

404. Brüggemann, Fritz. *Die Ironie als entwicklungsgeschichtliches Moment: Ein Beitrag zur Vorgeschichte der deutschen Romantik.* Jena: Eugen Diederichs, 1909. viii + 478 pp.

   Places *Lovell* into a line of novels including Goethe's *Werther*, Jacobi's *Woldemar*, and Moritz's *Anton Reiser*, all of which have "Probleme des Seelenlebens" as well as irony at their core.

405. Corkhill, Alan. "Perspectives on Language in Ludwig Tieck's Epistolary Novel *William Lovell*." *GQ*, 58 (1985): 173-183.

   Not unlike no. 421, concludes that, taken together, the disparate perspectives on language expressed by the correspondents in *Lovell* point to a definite "Sprachskepsis" on Tieck's part.

406. Esselborn, Hans. "Der 'Nihilismus' in Ludwig Tiecks 'William Lovell': Ein Beitrag zur Gattungsfrage." *WW*, 40 (1990): 4-22.

   From a structural standpoint, *Lovell* is inconsistent because it shifts abruptly from a pietistic epistolary novel to a story about human corruption.

407. Francke, Kuno. "The Social Aspect of Early German Romanticism." *PMLA*, 10 (1895): 83-96.

   An antagonistic essay describing *Lovell*, among other German romantic works, as the product of "an eccentric and uncontrolled imagination."

408. Guretzky-Cornitz, Ulrike von. *Versuch einer sozialpsychologischen Interpretation des psychologischen*

*Romans von Ludwig Tieck: "William Lovell."* Paderborn: Author, 1977. 233 pp.

*Lovell* is a psychological novel, in which Tieck attacks the amorality and hypocrisy of eighteenth century European society.

409. Hassler, Karl. *Ludwig Tiecks Jugendroman William Lovell und der Paysan perverti des Restif de la Bretonne.* Greifswald: Julius Abel, 1902. 167 pp.

A thorough and well-documented study concerning an important source for *Lovell* (see also nos. 411 and 412).

410. Herzog, Wilhelm. "Paris in Kleists Briefen und in Tiecks 'William Lovell.'" *Euphorion*, 15 (1908): 713-716.

The letters written by characters in *Lovell*, much like Heinrich von Kleist's personal letters, express a clear dislike for the city of Paris in particular and for urban landscapes in general (compare with nos. 142 and 420).

411. Jost, François. "Ludwig Tieck: English and French Sources of his William Lovell (1795/96)." *Studies in Eighteenth-Century Culture: Proceedings of the American Society for Eighteenth-Century Studies*, 2 (1972): 181-193.

Tieck fused raw materials from Ben Jonson's *The New Inn or the Light Heart* (1631) and Restif de la Bretonne's *Paysan perverti* (1775) into a "homogeneous compound" when he created *Lovell*. Nos. 409 and 412 contain additional information on sources.

412. ___. "Tiegel Tieck: 'William Lovell' et 'Le Paysan perverti.'" *EG*, 28 (1973): 29-48.

Similar to nos. 409 and 411.

413. Kimpel, Dieter. "Entstehung und Formen des Briefromans in Deutschland: Interpretationen zur Geschichte einer epischen Gattung des 18. Jahrhunderts und zur Entstehung des modernen deutschen Romans." Diss. Vienna, 1961.

Contains an informative section on the epistolary form of *Lovell*.

414. Knopper, Françoise. "L'image et le rôle de l'Italie dans *William Lovell* (1795) de Ludwig Tieck." *RGer*, 4 (1974): 3-15.

On the role of Italy in *Lovell*. For information concerning the portrayal of Italy in Tieck's poems, see no. 168.

415. ___. "L'Angleterre vue par le jeune Tieck: Une étude du roman épistolaire *William Lovell* (1795)." *RGer*, 8 (1978): 3-19.

A pendant to the preceding item.

416. Maelsaeke, Dirk van. "Experimentelle Romane der Goethezeit: Der Weimarer *Werther*, Stendhals *Le Rouge et le Noir* und Tiecks *William Lovell*." *ActaG*, 10 (1977): 213-243.

All three novels are discussed as important precursors of the *nouveau roman*, especially since they deal with modern existential questions.

417. Münz, Walter. *Individuum und Symbol in Tiecks "William Lovell": Materialien zum frühromantischen Subjektivismus*. Regensburger Beiträge zur deutschen Sprach- und Literaturwissenschaft, Series B: Untersuchungen, Vol. 2. Frankfurt/M., Berne: Peter Lang, 1975. 338 pp.

While detailed, this psychological and structural analysis of *Lovell* is rather unfocused.

418. Pikulik, Lothar. "Die Frühromantik in Deutschland als Ende und Anfang: Über Tiecks *William Lovell* und Friedrich Schlegels Fragmente." Pp. 112-128 in *Die literarische Frühromantik*, ed. Silvio Vietta. Kleine Vandenhoeck-Reihe, Vol. 1488. Göttingen: Vandenhoeck & Ruprecht, 1983. 223 pp.

Although *Lovell* is filled with a deep pessimism characteristic of late eighteenth century literature, it already clears the way for Tieck's romantic works via its protagonist's "Glauben an das Wunderbare."

419. Proskauer, Paul F. "Ludwig Tieck's *William Lovell* and Young Hugo von Hofmannsthal." *MAL*, 3, No. 3 (1970): 36-46.

Much like the young Hofmannsthal, Lovell is an alienated individual, "haunted by visions of the void and of nothingness," who is seeking an identity.

420. Riha, Karl. *Die Beschreibung der "Großen Stadt": Zur Entstehung des Großstadtmotivs in der deutschen Literatur (ca. 1750 - ca. 1850)*. Frankfurter Beiträge zur Germanistik, Vol. 11. Bad Homburg v.d.H., Berlin, Zurich: Gehlen, 1970. 182 pp.

On pp. 126-132 of this survey, Riha shows that the negative portrayal of Paris in *Lovell* was influenced by contemporary travelogues and that Tieck's account, for its part, influenced Kleist and other authors (see also nos. 142 and 410).

421. Scharnowski, Susanne. "Emphase und Skepsis: Ludwig Tiecks 'William Lovell' und Clemens Brentanos 'Godwi' als Briefromane." *WW*, 40 (1990): 22-32.

The named works signify the end of the epistolary tradition in eighteenth century Germany because the letters they contain are no longer powerful enough to convey the deeper feelings of the tormented protagonists (compare with no. 405).

422. Scheck, Ulrich. "The Hermetic Self and the Creative Reader: Metanarrative Discourse in Tieck's *William Lovell*." *Seminar*, 25 (1989): 95-103.

Concludes that "the multiperspectivism of Tieck's epistolary novel provides the ideal narrative structure for its hermeneutic message."

423. Thalmann, Marianne. *Der Trivialroman des 18. Jahrhunderts und der romantische Roman: Ein Beitrag zur Entwicklungsgeschichte der Geheimbundmystik*. Germanische Studien, Vol. 24. Berlin: Emil Ebering, 1923. 323 pp. Reprinted Nendeln/Liechtenstein: Kraus, 1967.

A precursor to the next item, this study demonstrates the close ties between *Lovell* and German trivial literature of the eighteenth century. For related analyses, refer to nos. 256, 278, and 279.

424. ___. *Die Romantik des Trivialen: Von Grosses "Genius" bis Tiecks "William Lovell."* List Taschenbücher der Wissenschaft, Vol. 1442. Munich: List, 1970. 138 pp.

Building on the preceding item, this monograph places *Lovell* into the context of trivial literature not only because it exemplifies "die fließenden Grenzen zwischen hoher und niedriger Literatur," but also because it leans toward "die Darstellung des Verbrecherischen, aber auch menschlich Interessanten" (see also nos. 256, 278, and 279).

425. Trainer, James. "William Lovell: Tieck's World of Chaos." *EG*, 23 (1968): 191-201.

Writing *Lovell* represented a type of "cathartic process" for Tieck because, in doing so, he could purge himself of "hypochondriac reflections and anarchistic inclinations" by transferring them to his ficticious hero.

426. Weigand, Karlheinz. "Offenbarung oder Chaos? Anmerkungen zum Naturverhältnis in Tiecks 'William Lovell.'" *JWGV*, 75 (1971): 41-56.

In *Lovell*, nature provides solace to a protagonist who experiences existential terror in a chaotic world. It thus possesses a romantic quality characteristic of Tieck's later works.

427. ___. *Tiecks "William Lovell": Studie zur frühromantischen Antithese*. Beiträge zur neueren Literaturgeschichte, N.S. 3, Vol. 23. Heidelberg: Carl Winter, 1975. 196 pp.

Through its epistolary form, *Lovell* attempts to express "die Überzeugung von der Mehrdeutigkeit der Welt wie des Einzellebens."

428. Wüstling, Fritz. *Tiecks William Lovell: Ein Beitrag zur Geistesgeschichte des 18. Jahrhunderts*. Bausteine zur Geschichte der neueren deutschen Literatur, Vol. 7. Halle a.S.: Max Niemeyer, 1912. xi + 192 pp.

Of particular interest is Wüstling's division of the novel's main characters into three distinct groups: "Egoisten und Freigeister," "Schwärmer," and "ausgeglichene Charaktere," whereby the last group is representative of Tieck's personal philosophy.

Cross ref.: 1, 113, 114, 159, 162, 234, 242, 251, 253, 396-402, 675, 720.


c. *Peter Lebrecht* (1795-1796)

429. Hering, Christoph. "Die Poetisierung des Alltäglichen in Tiecks 'Peter Lebrecht.'" *Monatshefte*, 49 (1957): 361-370.

The realistic elements in *Peter Lebrecht* foreshadow much of what was to come in Tieck's later novellas.

### d. *Franz Sternbalds Wanderungen* (1798)

430. Brömel, Karl. *Ludwig Tiecks Kunstanschauungen im "Sternbald."* Weida i. Thür.: Thomas & Hubert, 1928. 74 pp.

    Summarizes the novel's passages dealing with art (see also nos. 434 and 437).

431. Danton, G.H. "The Date of the Scene of Tieck's *Sternbald.*" *MLN*, 25 (1910): 11.

    Events in the work defy accurate dating because, on the whole, Tieck did not adhere to historical fact (compare with nos. 436 and 447).

432. Fink, Gonthier-Louis. "L'ambiguïté du message romantique dans *Franz Sternbalds Wanderungen* de L. Tieck." *RGer*, 4 (1974): 16-70.

    Tieck's attitude toward artists in *Sternbald* seems relatively ambiguous, since these individuals (e.g., Dürer and Michelangelo) are not clearly aligned with any sort of romantic idealism (contrast with no. 448).

433. Geulen, Hans. "Zeit und Allegorie im Erzählvorgang von Tiecks Roman 'Franz Sternbalds Wanderungen.'" *GRM*, 49 (1968): 281-298.

    Proves that *Sternbald* exhibits a great deal of structural unity via "das Einswerden von Vergangenheit und Zukunft, Erinnerung und Ahnung, Welt und Ich, Traum und Wirklichkeit" (compare with no. 439).

434. Harnisch, Käthe. *Deutsche Malererzählungen: Die Art des Sehens bei Heinse, Tieck, Hoffmann, Stifter*

*und Keller.* Neue deutsche Forschungen, Vol. 13. Berlin: Junker & Dünnhaupt, 1938. 106 pp.

Pp. 29-46 of this useful survey summarize Tieck's views on art, artists, and artistic perception as they emerge from *Sternbald* (see also nos. 430 and 437).

435. Hibberd, J.L. "The Idylls in Tieck's *Sternbald.*" *Forum for Modern Language Studies*, 12 (1976): 236-249.

Supports conclusions reached in no. 99 by stating that, through its break with the idyllic tradition, *Sternbald* symbolizes Tieck's transition from enlightened to romantic thought.

436. Hoermann, Roland. "Historicity and Art in Tieck's 'Sternbald.'" *Monatshefte*, 47 (1955): 209-220.

In direct contradiction to no. 431, maintains that Tieck did not stray far from historical fact in his portrayal of famous artists and their works (see also no. 447).

437. Kamphausen, A. "Tiecks 'Sternbalds Wanderungen': Einige Bemerkungen zu einem Zeugnis von Kunstanschauung." *Zeitschrift des deutschen Vereins für Kunstwissenschaft*, 3 (1936): 404-420.

General commentary on the role of art and the artist in *Sternbald*. More on this topic can be found in nos. 430 and 434).

438. Kempf, Thomas. "Ludwig Tieck: *Franz Sternbalds Wanderungen.* Zur Dialektik autonomieästhetischer Kunstkonzeption." *NG*, 4, No. 1 (1985): 7-40.

Discusses the relationship of art and society in *Sternbald* and bases many arguments on Herbert Marcuse's concept of "die affirmative Kultur."

439. Lillyman, W.J. "Der Erzähler und das Bild des Stromes in *Franz Sternbalds Wanderungen*." *GRM*, 52 (1971): 378-395. Revised version pp. 61-76 in no. 246.

   Utilizes the function of the narrator and the recurring image of the stream to demonstrate that *Sternbald* is characterized not by a fragmented, but rather by a highly ordered structure (see also no. 433).

440. Meuthen, Erich. "'...Denn er selbst war hier anders...': Zum Problem des Identitätsverlusts in Ludwig Tiecks *Sternbald*-Roman." *JDSG*, 30 (1986): 383-403.

   A language study pointing to ambiguities in *Sternbald*, which disorient both the protagonist and the reader.

441. Mornin, Edward. "Art and Alienation in Tieck's *Franz Sternbalds Wanderungen*." *MLN*, 94 (1979): 510-523.

   Sternbald's experiences show that "art may lead the artist to a false world-view and moral insensitivity."

442. ___. "Tieck's Revision of *Franz Sternbalds Wanderungen*." *Seminar*, 15 (1979): 79-96.

   Compares in detail the 1798 and 1843 versions of the novel, particularly with respect to content.

443. Prodnigg, Heinrich. "Über Tiecks Sternbald und sein Verhältnis zu Goethes Wilhelm Meister." *Jahrbuch der Steiermärkischen Landes-Oberrealschule in Graz*, 41 (1892): 3-21.

   Tieck's "Bildungsroman" is heavily indebted to Goethe, especially in terms of motifs and characters. More on this topic in nos. 237 and 243.

444. Ribbat, Ernst. "Ludwig Tieck: *Franz Sternbalds Wanderungen* (1798)." Pp. 58-74 in *Romane und Erzählungen der deutschen Romantik: Neue Interpretatio-*

*nen*, ed. Paul Michael Lützeler. Stuttgart: Philipp Reclam jun., 1981. 389 pp.

Interprets *Sternbald* as "eine Dichtung der Revolutionsepoche" because it deviates from traditional modes of perception and thought.

445. Roetteken, Hubert. "Die Charaktere in Tiecks Roman 'Franz Sternbalds Wanderungen.'" *Zeitschrift für vergleichende Literaturgeschichte*, N.S. 6 (1893): 188-242.

The novel's major characters are examined in light of their aesthetic and historical functions.

446. Sammons, Jeffrey L. "Tieck's *Franz Sternbald*: The Loss of Thematic Control." *SIR*, 5 (1965/66): 30-43.

Speculates that Tieck did not complete *Sternbald* because he had lost track of the "original forming principle" underlying the work.

447. Schmidt, Thomas E. *Die Geschichtlichkeit des frühromantischen Romans: Literarische Reaktion auf Erfahrungen eines kulturellen Wandels*. Studien zur deutschen Literatur, Vol. 105. Tübingen: Max Niemeyer, 1989. vi + 283 pp.

On pp. 36-98, Schmidt argues that *Sternbald* was not intended as any sort of accurate historical portrayal, but instead as a "Literarisierung der kulturphilosophischen Option der 'Herzensergießungen.'" Contributes to the discussion in nos. 431 and 436.

448. Schulz, Eberhard Wilhelm. "Der mittelalterliche Künstler in Tiecks Roman 'Franz Sternbalds Wanderungen.'" Pp. 35-48 in Schulz, *Wort und Zeit: Aufsätze und Vorträge zur Literaturgeschichte*. Kieler Studien zur deutschen Literaturgeschichte, Vol. 6. Neumünster: Karl Wachholtz, 1968. 288 pp.

In contrast to Fink (no. 432), Schulz maintains that the medieval artist, symbolized by Albrecht Dürer, represents "die von der Romantik immer wieder ausgesprochene Idealvorstellung einer heilsam gebundenen Menschenordnung und Kunst."

Cross ref.: 113, 115, 159, 256, 396-402, 453, 621, 623, 689, 702, 703.

### e. *Der Aufruhr in den Cevennen* (1826)

449. Lebede, Hans. *Tiecks Novelle "Der Aufruhr in den Cevennen": Eine literarhistorische Untersuchung.* Halle a.S.: Max Niemeyer, 1909. xii + 222 pp.

    A comprehensive introduction to the novel focusing on sources, underlying historical events, plot, characters, and the role of religion. Represents a substantial revision of and expansion upon Lebede's published dissertation: *Tiecks Novelle "Der Aufruhr in den Cevennen": Beiträge zur Erforschung ihrer Quellen.* Berlin: Plahn, 1906. 47 pp.

450. Porterfield, Allen W. "Tieck's *Aufruhr in den Cevennen*." *GQ*, 7 (1934): 58-69.

    Attacks Tieck for being an armchair romantic, of sorts, who never visited the Cevennes mountains and whose description of them is correspondingly dull and lifeless.

451. Richter, Fritz K. "Ludwig Tieck's Novel about the Camisard Revolt in the Cevennes Mountains." *The Shaker Quarterly*, 14 (1974): 3-11.

    An introduction for the layman.

452. Wenger, Karl. *Historische Dramen deutscher Romantiker (Untersuchung über den Einfluss Walter Scotts).* Untersuchungen zur neueren Sprach- und Literaturgeschichte, Vol. 7. Berne: A. Francke, 1905. vii + 123 pp.

Pp. 90-121 are devoted primarily to Scott's influence on *Cevennen*. Acknowledges that Tieck and Scott held widely differing views concerning history, its portrayal and significance.

### f. *Vittoria Accorombona* (1840)

453. Keck, Christiane E. *Renaissance and Romanticism: Tieck's conception of Cultural Decline as Portrayed in his "Vittoria Accorombona."* German Studies in America, Vol. 20. Berne, Frankfurt/M.: Herbert Lang, 1976. 120 pp.

   In contrast to Franz Sternbald, the heroine of this novel is no longer rooted in German romantic idealism expressed through some "imaginary context of historical grandeur," but rather portrays the actual spirit and culture of Italy as it existed during the Renaissance (compare with nos. 456 and 462).

454. Landau, Marcus. "Vittoria Accorombona in der Dichtung im Verhältnis zu ihrer wahren Geschichte." *Euphorion*, 9 (1902): 310-316.

   Reports on the historical events surrounding Vittoria Accorombona's life and evaluates the degree to which John Webster and Tieck adhered to them in their respective works *The White Devil* (1612) and *Accorombona* (see also nos. 459 and 674).

455. Lillyman, W.J. "Ludwig Tieck's *Vittoria Accorombona*." *JEGP*, 70 (1971): 468-487. Revised version pp. 131-154 in no. 246.

   A structural analysis focusing on the novel's metaphors, images, patterns of events, and characters as well as on the arrangement of its chapters and on the role of its narrator. Clearly shows that *Accorombona* is a homogeneous work of art worthy of critical consideration.

456. Mörtl, Hans. "Die Renaissance in Tiecks 'Vittoria Accorombona.'" *Neue Jahrbücher für das klassische Altertum, Geschichte und deutsche Literatur und für Pädagogik*, 26 (1923): 89-106.

Much like Weibel (no. 462), and in contrast to Keck (no. 453), views *Accorombona* as a late work of Romanticism that does not provide an accurate portrayal of the Renaissance period.

457. Rehm, Walther. *Das Werden des Renaissancebildes in der deutschen Dichtung vom Rationalismus bis zum Realismus*. Munich: C.H. Beck, 1924. 192 pp.

Lauds *Accorombona* as the best and most colorful German "Renaissancedichtung" until the appearance of C.F. Meyer's works.

458. Schütz, Wilhelm von. *Über den katholischen Charakter der antiken Tragödie und die neuesten Versuche der Herren Tieck, Tölken und Böckh dieselbe zu dekatholisiren*. Mainz: Kirchheim, Schott & Thielmann, 1842. 78 pp.

An attack, mounted by a catholic apologist, against perceived protestant tendencies in *Accorombona* and other works of the time.

459. Siegel, Paul Gerhard. "Ludwig Tiecks 'Vittoria Accorombona' und ihre Quellen." *Jahrbuch der Philosophischen Fakultät zu Leipzig*, 1923, pp. 45-47. Excerpt of Diss. Leipzig, 1923.

On the historical and literary sources for *Accorombona* (compare with nos. 454 and 674).

460. Taraba, Wolfgang F. "Tieck: Vittoria Accorombona." Pp. 329-352 in *Der deutsche Roman vom Barock bis zur Gegenwart: Struktur und Geschichte*, Vol. 1, ed. Benno von Wiese. Düsseldorf: August Bagel, 1963. 442 pp.

A general introduction with commentary on the novel's psychological depth and importance for German literature.

461. Viëtor, Karl. "Tieck oder Kleist?" *Jahrbuch der Kleist-Gesellschaft*, 1925/26, pp. 138-147. Shortened version in *Frankfurter Zeitung*, Frankfurt, 26 August 1926, p. 1.

Confirms Tieck's authorship of *Accorombona*.

462. Weibel, Oskar. *Tiecks Renaissancedichtung in ihrem Verhältnis zu Heinse und C.F. Meyer.* Sprache und Dichtung, Vol. 34. Berne: Paul Haupt, 1925. 167 pp.

*Accorombona*, forming a thematic link between Heinse's *Ardinghello* (1787) and the novellas of C.F. Meyer, is a distinctly romantic work on the basis of the subjective portrayal of its heroine (compare with nos. 453 and 456).

Cross ref.: 398, 402, 711.

# VII. Criticism: Letters

## 1. GENERAL

463. Littlejohns, Richard. "Die Briefsammlung Ludwig Tiecks: Zur Entstehung eines literaturgeschichtlichen Problems." *Aurora*, 47 (1987): 159-175.

On the fate of Tieck's personal letter collection, which numbered 2,690 items in 1852.

464. Zeydel, Edwin H. "Nachträge zu Holteis *Briefe an Tieck*." *MLN*, 43 (1928): 459-464.

Criticism of no. 467, including correction of various mistakes.

465. ___. "Die Briefe Ludwig Tiecks: Ein literarisches Problem." *JEGP*, 28 (1929): 72-85.

Lists all letters written by Tieck that were published as of 1929. Useful.

466. ___ and Percy Matenko. "A Supplementary List of Published Letters from and to Tieck." *GR*, 5 (1930): 182-183.

An addendum to the preceding two items.

## 2. COLLECTIONS ENCOMPASSING NUMEROUS CORRESPONDENTS

467. Holtei, Karl von, ed. *Briefe an Ludwig Tieck*. Breslau: Eduard Trewendt, 1864. 4 vols. xvi + 376, 368, 384, 366 pp.

An enormous collection of letters received by Tieck from correspondents including Arnim, Brentano, Grabbe, Hebbel, E.T.A. Hoffmann, Immermann, Kerner, Laube, Lenz, Ludwig, Menzel, Mörike, Nicolai, Novalis, Prutz, the Schlegels, Schwab, Steffens, Ticknor, Varnhagen von Ense, and Wackenroder. Located at the Tieck archive in Berlin, the letters are arranged alphabetically and are accompanied by useful commentary (to which corrections are made in no. 464). The collection also includes nine letters written by Tieck. No. 473 represents a companion work to the present volumes, in that it contains a large collection of letters stemming from Tieck's hand.

468. ___, ed. *Dreihundert Briefe aus zwei Jahrhunderten*. Hannover: Karl Rümpler, 1872. 4 parts in 2 vols. xxii + 171, 226, xvi + 183, 159 pp. Reprinted Berne: Lang, 1971.

Contains one letter written by Georg Reinbeck to Tieck on 25 June 1846, seven letters from Tieck to Wackenroder (all dated 1792), one letter from Tieck to J.P. LePique dated 21 November 1803, and one unaddressed and undated letter by Tieck.

469. Matenko, Percy. "A Short Supplement to the Letters of Ludwig Tieck." *GR*, 24 (1949): 18-20.

Presentation of three letters omitted in no. 473.

470. ___, Edwin H. Zeydel, and Bertha Masche, eds. *Letters to and from Ludwig Tieck and his Circle: Unpublished Letters from the Period of German Romanticism Including the Unpublished Correspondence of Sophie and Ludwig Tieck.* University of North Carolina Studies in the Germanic Languages and Literatures, Vol. 57. Chapel Hill: The University of North Carolina Press, 1967. xxiii + 394 pp.

A supplement to no. 473.

471. Schweikert, Uwe. "Korrespondenzen Ludwig Tiecks und seiner Geschwister: 68 unveröffentlichte Briefe." *JFDH*, 1971, pp. 311-429.

Newly found additions to the correspondence of Tieck and his siblings Friedrich and Sophie. The collection, continued in the next item, contains letters to and from such noted individuals as Bettina Brentano, Carus, Maler Müller, and Felix Mendelssohn-Bartholdy.

472. ___. "Korrespondenzen Ludwig Tiecks: 16 unveröffentlichte Briefe." *JFDH*, 1974, pp. 245-280.

A continuation of the preceding item.

473. Zeydel, Edwin H., Percy Matenko, and Robert Herndon Fife, eds. *Letters of Ludwig Tieck Hitherto Unpublished 1792-1853.* New York: Modern Language Association of America; London: Oxford University Press, 1937. xxxi + 604 pp. Reprinted Millwood, N.Y.: Kraus, 1973.

This collection, a pendant to no. 467, is primarily composed of letters written by Tieck to his German correspondents (e.g., his father, siblings Friedrich and Sophie, Asher, Theodor von Bernhardi, Carus, Cotta, König Friedrich Wilhelm IV. von Preußen, Frommann, Holtei, Küstner, Max, Nicolai, Reimer, Rumohr, Steffens, Wackenroder, and Winkler). Arranged chronologically and accompanied by helpful commentary. Supplemented by nos. 469 and 470.

## 3. LETTERS TO/FROM INDIVIDUAL CORRESPONDENTS

### a. Friedrich and Sophie Tieck

474. Klee, Gotthold. "Tiecks Reise von Berlin nach Erlangen 1793, von ihm selbst berichtet." Pp. 180-190 in *Forschungen zur deutschen Philologie: Festgabe für Rudolf Hildebrand zum 13. März 1894*. Leipzig: Veit & Comp., 1894. 324 pp.

    A letter from Tieck to Sophie dated 2 May 1793, in which he gives a detailed account of his travels.

475. ___. "Ein Brief Ludwig Tiecks aus Jena vom 6. Dezember 1799." *Euphorion*, Supplemental Vol. 3 (1897): 211-215.

    Addressed to Sophie.

476. Trainer, James. "Anatomy of a Debt: Friedrich 'Maler' Müller and the Tiecks. With Unpublished Correspondence." *OGS*, 11 (1980): 146-177.

    Uses newly discovered Tieck family letters from the years 1806-1823 to document that Ludwig and Friedrich Tieck were caught in the middle of a financially motivated conflict between their sister Sophie and the writer Maler Müller.

477. ___. "Sophie an Ludwig Tieck: Neu identifizierte Briefe." *JDSG*, 24 (1980): 162-181.

    Five letters, of which only one is dated.

Cross ref.: 471, 472, 624.

## b. Goethe

478. Schüddekopf, Carl and Oskar Walzel. "Goethes Briefwechsel mit Ludwig Tieck." Pp. 290-312, 378-382 in Schüddekopf and Walzel, eds., *Goethe und die Romantik: Briefe mit Erläuterungen*, Vol. 1. Schriften der Goethe-Gesellschaft, Vol. 13. Weimar: Goethe-Gesellschaft, 1898. xcv + 382 pp.

A collection of eleven letters from Tieck to Goethe and seven letters from Goethe to Tieck, all from the years 1798-1829. With commentary on pp. 378-382.

## c. Jean Paul

479. Förster, Ernst, ed. *Wahrheit aus Jean Paul's Leben*, Vol. 7. Breslau: Josef Max, 1833. xiv + 368 pp.

Contains, on pp. 53-55, an excerpt of a letter from Jean Paul to Tieck dated 5 October 1805 and, on pp. 290-292, a complete letter from Tieck to Jean Paul written on 17 June 1812.

480. Schweikert, Uwe. "Jean Paul und Ludwig Tieck: Mit einem ungedruckten Brief Tiecks an Jean Paul." *JJPG*, 8 (1973): 23-77.

A letter from Tieck to Jean Paul dated 12 August 1821 forms the basis of this article dealing with the friendship existing between the two men since 1798.

481. Wolff, Kurt. "Drei ungedruckte Briefe von Tieck an Jean Paul Friedrich Richter." *Münchner Neueste Nachrichten*, Munich, Supplement no. 11, 12 July 1908.

Three newly discovered letters from the years 1822-1824.

### d. Romantic Generation

*i*. The Schlegels
(August Wilhelm, Dorothea, Friedrich)

482. Finke, Heinrich, ed. *Briefe an Friedrich Schlegel*. Cologne: J.P. Bachem, 1917. 104 pp.

   Includes, on pp. 92-96, two letters from Tieck to Dorothea dated 1829 and one to Friedrich from 15 July 1822.

483. Körner, Josef, ed. *Krisenjahre der Frühromantik: Briefe aus dem Schlegelkreis*, 2nd ed. Berne, Munich: Francke, 1969. 2 vols. xxiv + 669, 567 pp.

   Vol. 1 contains a letter from Tieck to A.W. Schlegel dated 8 October 1804 (p. 160) and a letter from A.W. Schlegel to Tieck dated 13 June 1808 (p. 535). Both volumes include numerous pieces of correspondence between A.W. Schlegel and Friedrich and Sophie Tieck.

484. Lohner, Edgar, ed. *Ludwig Tieck und die Brüder Schlegel: Briefe. Auf der Grundlage der von Henry Lüdeke besorgten Edition neu herausgegeben und kommentiert*. Winkler Texte. Munich: Winkler, 1972. 275 pp.

   A continuation of the next item.

485. Lüdeke, H., ed. *Ludwig Tieck und die Brüder Schlegel: Briefe mit Einleitung und Anmerkungen*. Ottendorfer Memorial Fellowship Series of New York University, Vol. 13. Frankfurt am Main: Joseph Baer, 1930. 252 pp.

   This critical edition of the correspondence between Tieck and the Schlegels is expanded upon in the preceding item.

486. Wieneke, Ernst, ed. *Caroline und Dorothea Schlegel in Briefen*. Weimar: G. Kiepenheuer, 1914. 596 pp.

On p. 543, includes a letter from Dorothea to Tieck dated 15 July 1829.

487. Zeydel, Edwin H. "An Unpublished Letter of Dorothea Schlegel to Ludwig Tieck." *GR*, 17 (1942): 56-61.

Letter postmarked 15 April 1829.

Cross ref.: 587, 606.

### *ii*. Wackenroder

488. Fambach, Oscar. "Zum Briefwechsel Wilhelm Heinrich Wackenroders mit Ludwig Tieck." *JFDH*, 1968, pp. 257-282.

Provides correct dates and commentary for all known letters.

489. Leyen, Friedrich von der, ed. *Wilhelm Heinrich Wackenroder: Werke und Briefe*, Vol. 2. Jena: Eugen Diederichs, 1910. 257 pp.

The correspondence between Tieck and Wackenroder, consisting of 27 letters written in the period 1792-1794, is presented here in unified form for the first time after being published in separate sources (see no. 467 for Wackenroder's letters, and no. 468 for those of Tieck).

490. Littlejohns, Richard. "Zum Briefwechsel zwischen Wackenroder und Tieck: Einige Berichtigungen und Bemerkungen." *ZDP*, 97 (1978): 616-624.

Editorial commentary vis-à-vis the Tieck-Wackenroder letters, especially as printed in nos. 467 and 468.

*iii.* Others
(Arnim, Görres, Jakob Grimm, E.T.A. Hoffmann,
Kerner, Runge, Uhland)

491. Binder, Franz, ed. *Joseph von Görres: Gesammelte Briefe*, Vol. 2: *Freundesbriefe (1802-1821)*. Munich: In Commission der literarisch-artistischen Anstalt, 1874. xxxvii + 646 pp.

Pp. 600-601 contain a letter from Tieck to Görres dated 24 December 1819 that was brought to its recipient by a Scotsman wrongly identified by Tieck as Damatyne. For a clarification of this error, see no. 61.

492. Hartmann, Julius, ed. *Uhlands Briefwechsel, im Auftrag des Schwäbischen Schillervereins*, Vol. 2. Stuttgart: J.G. Cotta, 1912. xii + 457 pp.

A letter from Tieck to Uhland (no place or date) can be found on p. 448.

493. Kerner, Theobald, ed. *Justinus Kerners Briefwechsel mit seinen Freunden*, Vol. 2. Stuttgart, Leipzig: Deutsche Verlags-Anstalt, 1897. vi + 554 pp.

Includes three letters from Tieck to Kerner dated 22 May 1841, 3 July 1841, and 16 March 1853. Same letters in no. 48.

494. [Runge, Johann Daniel], ed. *Philipp Otto Runge: Hinterlassene Schriften*. Hamburg: Friedrich Perthes, 1840-1841. 2 vols. 435, xii + 554 pp.

Vol. 1 contains three letters from Runge to Tieck (pp. 23-28, 39-42, 60-61). Vol. 2 contains one letter from Runge to Tieck (p. 349), two letters from Tieck to Runge (pp. 206-207, 262-264) as well as one letter from Tieck to the editor of the present volumes (p. 437). The above letters range in date from 1803-1807, with the exception of the last, which is dated 1812.

495. Segebrecht, Wulf. "Ludwig Tieck an E.T.A. Hoffmann: Ein bisher unpublizierter Brief vom 12. August 1820." *Mitteilungen der E.T.A. Hoffmann-Gesellschaft*, 32 (1986): 1-11.

First publication of a newly discovered letter.

496. Stengel, E. "Zwei Briefe Jakob Grimms an Ludwig Tieck und Clemens Brentano sowie ein Briefchen von Clemens Brentano an und ein Zeugnis Savignys für Jakob Grimm." Pp. 150-156 in *Festschrift Wilhelm Viëtor zum 25. Dezember 1910. Die neueren Sprachen*, Supplemental Vol. for 1910. Marburg: N.G. Elwert, 1910. 333 pp.

Letter from Grimm to Tieck postmarked 18 April 1808.

497. Weiss, Hermann, ed. *Unbekannte Briefe von und an Achim von Arnim aus der Sammlung Varnhagen und anderen Beständen*. Schriften zur Literaturwissenschaft, Vol. 4. Berlin: Duncker & Humblot, 1986. 357 pp.

Pp. 73-75 hold a 13 February 1827 Arnim to Tieck letter.

Cross ref.: 74 (Oehlenschläger).

e. **Dresden Circle**

*i*. Böttiger

498. Geiger, Ludwig. "Ein Urteil über Bettinas Briefwechsel." *Goethe-Jahrbuch*, 15 (1894): 296-297.

A hitherto unpublished letter written by Tieck to Karl August Böttiger in 1835 concerning Bettina von Arnim's *Goethes Briefwechsel mit einem Kinde*.

499. Körner, Jos. "Ludwig Tieck über 'Goethes Briefwechsel mit einem Kinde.'" *ZDP*, 55 (1930): 390-391.

Same letter as in the preceding item, of which Körner was obviously not aware. However, in an addendum to the present article [*ZDP*, 56 (1931): 128] a more precise date is supplied for the letter, namely 10-11 July 1835.

### *ii*. Carus

500. Kurrelmeyer, W. "Another Letter from Tieck to Carus." *MLN*, 43 (1928): 308-309.

    First printing of an invitation received by Carus to attend Tieck's reading of *King Lear* on 28 October 1827.

501. Zeydel, Edwin H. "The Relations of Ludwig Tieck and K.G. Carus (With Four Unpublished Letters)."*MLN*,43 (1928): 73-78.

    Illustrates Tieck's close friendship with Carus via four letters from the Dresden years.

### *iii*. Others
(Bülow, Prinz Johann von Sachsen, Laun, Ida von Lüttichau, Uechtritz)

502. Etscheit, Lotte. "An Unpublished Letter from Ludwig Tieck to Philalethes." *GR*, 12 (1937): 14-16.

    Tieck thanks Prinz Johann von Sachsen for a copy of his Dante translation in a letter dated 23 July 1840.

503. Fiebiger, Otto, ed. *Ludwig Tieck und Ida von Lüttichau in ihren Briefen*. Mitteilungen des Vereins für Geschichte Dresdens, Vol. 32. Dresden-N.: C. Heinrich, 1937. 62 pp.

    The extant correspondence between Tieck and a devoted member of his Dresden circle.

504. Laun, Friedrich [Friedrich August Schulze]. *Gesammelte Schriften*, ed. Ludwig Tieck, Vol. 1. Stuttgart: Scheible, Rieger & Sattler, 1843. 465 pp.

A letter from Tieck to Laun concerning the composition of the latter's collected works. Laun incorporated this letter into the first volume of his collection as an introduction. Tieck later republished the letter as "Ein Brief an Friedrich Laun: 1842" on pp. 401-409 of his *Kritische Schriften*, Vol. 2. Leipzig: F.A. Brockhaus, 1848. vi + 424 pp.

505. Segebrecht, Wulf. "Ludwig Tieck an Eduard von Bülow: Dreiundzwanzig Briefe." *JFDH*, 1966, pp. 384-456.

23 letters by Tieck to his literary collaborator Eduard von Bülow, of which 22 were previously unpublished. The letters range in date from 1832-1851.

506. [Uechtritz, Maria], ed. *Erinnerungen an Friedrich von Uechtritz und seine Zeit in Briefen von ihm und an ihn*. Leipzig: S. Hirzel, 1884. xxxvi + 419 pp.

Pp. 145-162 contain six letters from Tieck to Uechtritz from the period 1825-1847.

Cross ref.: 42 (König Friedrich August II. von Sachsen).


### f. Raumer

507. Becker, Marta. "Unveröffentlichte Briefe Friedrich von Raumers an Ludwig Tieck." *Deutsche Rundschau*, 219 (1929): 144-157.

A find consisting of three letters dated 1827 and two that are undated.

508. Raumer, Friedrich von. *Lebenserinnerungen und Briefwechsel*. Leipzig: F.A. Brockhaus, 1861. 2 vols. viii + 286, viii + 377 pp.

Contains, in both volumes, the bulk of the correspondence between Tieck and Raumer. Supplemented by the next item.

509. ___. *Litterarischer Nachlaß*, Vol. 2. Berlin: Mittler und Sohn, 1869. ix + 321 pp.

Letters on pp. 139 ff. represent an addition to the preceding item.

510. Zeydel, Edwin H. and Percy Matenko. "Unpublished Letters of Ludwig Tieck to Friedrich von Raumer." *GR*, 5 (1930): 19-37, 147-165. Reprinted as *Ludwig Tieck-Friedrich von Raumer Letters: Hitherto Unpublished Letters from Ludwig Tieck to Friedrich von Raumer*, ed. Edwin H. Zeydel and Percy Matenko. Germanic Review Texts, Vol. 2. New York: Columbia University Press, 1930. 38 pp.

Eight newly discovered letters from the years 1816-1838.

**g. Actors**

*i.* Devrient

511. Houben, Heinrich Hubert. *Emil Devrient: Sein Leben, sein Wirken, sein Nachlaß. Ein Gedenkbuch*. Frankfurt am Main: Rütten & Loening, 1903. ix + 493 pp.

Contains three letters from Tieck to Devrient concerning the latter's stage performances. All undated, but Houben speculates that they were written in 1831, 1832, and 1833 respectively.

*ii.* Iffland

512. Dingelstedt, Franz, ed. *Johann Valentin Teichmanns literarischer Nachlaß*. Stuttgart: J.G. Cotta, 1863. xii + 466 pp.

First publication of the correspondence between Tieck and Iffland. Comprises five letters by Tieck and three by Iffland, all written during the period 1799-1800 and later acquired by Teichmann, who was active in the Berlin theater scene.

## h. Philosophers

### i. Fichte

513. Lauth, Reinhard and Hans Gliwitzky, eds. *Johann Gottlieb Fichte: Briefe*, Vol. 4: *Briefwechsel 1799-1800*. Stuttgart-Bad Cannstatt: Friedrich Frommann, 1973. 473 pp.

This collection of correspondence, which appears as Vol. 3, Part 4, of the J.G. Fichte *Gesamtausgabe* initiated in 1962 by Lauth and Gliwitzky, contains (on pp. 344-345) one letter from Fichte to Tieck dated October 1822.

### ii. Solger

514. Matenko, Percy, ed. *Tieck and Solger: The Complete Correspondence*. New York, Berlin: B. Westermann, 1933. xvi + 593 pp.

A collection of 104 letters between the two men ranging in date from 1811-1819. Accompanied by extensive commentary.

## i. Publishers

### i. Brockhaus

515. Lüdeke von Möllendorff, Heinrich, ed. *Aus Tiecks Novellenzeit: Briefwechsel zwischen Tieck und F.A. Brockhaus*. Leipzig: F.A. Brockhaus, 1928. vi + 221 pp.

Comprehensive collection with useful notes.

516. Matenko, Percy. "An Unpublished Letter from Ludwig Tieck to Brockhaus." *GR*, 4 (1929): 305-307.

An addition to the previous item dated 31 December 1847.

*ii*. Zimmer

517. Brinker-Gabler, Gisela. "Ludwig Tieck an Johann Georg Zimmer: Ein Beitrag zum Heldenbuch-Projekt." *JFDH*, 1974, pp. 235-244.

First complete transcription of a letter dated 11 October 1807.

518. Reichel, Otto. *Der Verlag von Mohr und Zimmer in Heidelberg und die Heidelberger Romantik*. Augsburg: Reichel, 1913. 114 pp.

Includes a fragment of a previously unpublished letter from Tieck to Zimmer dated 20 December 1807.

519. Zimmer, Heinrich W.B. *Johann Georg Zimmer und die Romantiker: Ein Beitrag zur Geschichte der Romantik, nebst bisher ungedruckten Briefen von Arnim, Böckh, Brentano, Görres, Marheineke, Fr. Perthes, J.C. Savigny, Brüder Schlegel, L. Tieck, de Wette u.A.* Frankfurt a.M.: Heyder und Zimmer, 1888. viii + 383 pp.

Pp. 260-266 contain three letters from Tieck to Zimmer, all from 1807.

*iii*. Others
(Cotta, Frommann, Göschen, Max, Reimer, Voß & Leo)

520. Fehling, Maria, ed. *Briefe an Cotta*, Vol. 1: *Das Zeitalter Goethes und Napoleons 1794-1815*. Stuttgart, Berlin: J.G. Cotta, 1925. x + 530 pp.

Five letters from Tieck to Cotta, dated 1800-1824, are located on pp. 247-255. See also no. 473.

521. Frommann, Friedrich Johannes. *Das Frommannsche Haus und seine Freunde*, 3rd ed. Stuttgart: F. Frommann, 1889. xxxii + 191 pp.

   Includes (on pp. 35-37) a letter from Tieck to the publisher's wife dated 28 April 1828. See also no. 473.

522. Geyder, August. "Einiges aus Briefen von Goethe, Steffens und Tieck an den Buchhändler Josef Max in Breslau." *Deutsches Museum: Zeitschrift für Literatur, Kunst und öffentliches Leben*, 14, Part 1 (1864): 888-895.

   Contains excerpts of four letters from Tieck to Max, the publisher of many of his later novellas. Two are undated, one is dated 14 March 1827, and the last 3 April 1828. This last letter is printed in its entirety in no. 473, which boasts a collection of 28 letters written by Tieck to Max in the years 1825-1842. See also no. 524.

523. Goldfriedrich, J., ed. *Aus den Briefen der Göschensammlung des Börsenvereins der deutschen Buchhändler zu Leipzig*. Leipzig: Gesellschaft der Freunde der Deutschen Bücherei, 1918. 71 pp.

   Lists one letter from Tieck to Göschen dated 23 February 1794.

524. Günther, H. "Ungedruckte Briefe L. Tiecks." *Euphorion*, 20 (1913): 641-647; and 21 (1914): 230-237.

   Four newly discovered letters from Tieck to the publishers Frommann, Max, and Voß & Leo from the period 1797-1833. For more on the Tieck-Frommann and Tieck-Max correspondence, see nos. 473 and 522.

525. Müller, Gustav Adolf, ed. *Stimmen toter Dichter: Briefe, Gedichte, Erinnerungen. Ein Gedenkbuch.* Hannover, Leipzig: O. Tobies, 1904. iv + 105 pp.

A letter written by Tieck to Reimer on 2 September 1802 is included. The full Tieck-Reimer collection can be found in no. 473. See also no. 594.

Cross ref.: 587 (Mohr).

### j. Correspondents Associated with Tieck's Editorial Projects

*i.* Anton von Hardenberg

526. Matenko, Percy and Richard Samuel. "Two Unpublished Tieck-Anton von Hardenberg Letters." *GR*, 32 (1957): 255-258.

Letters from Tieck to a relative of Novalis concerning publication of the latter's literary remains.

*ii.* Hartmann

527. Zeydel, Edwin H. "Der Maler Ferdinand Hartmann und Ludwig Tiecks Ausgabe der Schriften Kleists (Mit zwei unbekannten Briefen Tiecks)." *Jahrbuch der Kleist-Gesellschaft*, 17 (1937): 95-97.

Two letters from the year 1816 proving conclusively that Hartmann assisted Tieck in procuring materials for an edition of Heinrich von Kleist's works.

*iii.* Schlosser

528. Genton, Elisabeth. "Ein Brief Ludwig Tiecks über die nachgelassenen Schriften von Lenz." *Jahrbuch der Sammlung Kippenberg*, 1 (1963): 169-184.

Tieck solicits materials for his Lenz edition in this previously unpublished letter to J.F.H. Schlosser dated 8 January 1825.

### k. Foreign Correspondents

#### i. Coleridge

529. Coleridge, Ernest Hartley, ed. *Letters of Samuel Taylor Coleridge*, Vol. 2. Boston, New York: Houghton Mifflin and Co., 1895. vii + 813 pp.

    Contains, on p. 670, a letter from Tieck to Coleridge dated 30 April 1834, which is printed in English translation, as well as a summary of a letter written by Tieck to Coleridge on 20 February 1818. Concerning the latter, see next item.

530. Griggs, Earl Leslie. "Ludwig Tieck and Samuel Taylor Coleridge." *JEGP*, 54 (1955): 262-268.

    First complete transcription of the 20 February 1818 letter only summarized in the preceding item.

#### ii. Ticknor

531. Ticknor, Anna, ed. *Life, Letters and Journals of George Ticknor*, Vol. 2. Boston: J.R. Osgood & Co., 1876. vi + 533 pp.

    P. 260 holds a letter from Tieck to the American Hispanicist dated 28 July 1850 (printed in English translation).

#### iii. Austrians
(Bayer, Castelli, Matthäus von Collin, Deinhardstein, Karoline von Pichler, Schreyvogel)

532. "Bunte Reihe: Ungedruckte Briefe von Christian August Vulpius, Johann Ladislaus Pyrker, Ludwig Tieck, H.K.

Friedrich Peucer, Joh. Gabriel Seidl, Louis Schneider und Alfred Meißner." *Deutsche Dichtung*, 28 (1900): 289-294.

Contains, on pp. 291-292, a letter from Tieck to Deinhardstein postmarked 16 February 1853.

533. Körner, Josef. "Briefe von Ludwig Tieck." *Zeitschrift für Bücherfreunde*, N.S. 9 (1917): 156-162.

First publication of letters Tieck directed to Rudolf Bayer, Matthäus von Collin, Karoline von Pichler, and Schreyvogel. All written during the years 1813-1839.

534. Matenko, Percy. "Tieck and his Austrian Friends." *GR*, 17 (1942): 117-131.

Eight previously unpublished letters from the period 1813-1844, one each from Tieck to Rudolf Bayer, Matthäus von Collin, Deinhardstein, Karoline von Pichler, and Schreyvogel, one from Deinhardstein to Tieck, and two from Tieck to Castelli.

## l. Others

### *i*. Known Correspondents
(Bernhardi, Brinkman, Burgsdorff, Fritze, Grabbe, Gries, Hebbel, F.H. Jacobi, Klingemann, Köpke, Küstner, Menzel, Reuss, Riemer, Robert, Johanna Schopenhauer, Varnhagen von Ense, Wendt)

535. Assing, Ludmilla, ed. *Aus dem Nachlaß Varnhagen's von Ense: Briefe von Chamisso, Gneisenau, Haugwitz, W. von Humboldt, Prinz Louis Ferdinand, Rahel, Rückert, L. Tieck u.a. Nebst Briefen, Anmerkungen und Notizen von Varnhagen von Ense*, Vol. 1. Leipzig: F.A. Brockhaus, 1867. vii + 320 pp.

Contains (on pp. 189-239) a 1793 letter from Tieck to Bernhardi describing his travels through Franconia with Wackenroder, and (on pp. 239-242) a letter from Varnhagen to Tieck dated 1 July 1836.

536. Baldensperger, Fernand. "Un billet inédit de Tieck à Louis Robert." *RLC*, 7 (1927): 178.

An undated note written by Tieck to Ludwig Robert concerning one of the "Vorleseabende" in Dresden.

537. Bamberg, Felix, ed. *Friedrich Hebbels Briefwechsel mit Freunden und berühmten Zeitgenossen*, Vol. 1. Berlin: G. Grote, 1890. xiv + 460 pp.

Pp. 143-144 hold a letter from Tieck to Hebbel dated 23 January 1839 (concerns the latter's manuscript of *Schnock*) as well as Hebbel's reply written on 17 February 1840.

538. Bergmann, Alfred, ed. *Grabbe: Begegnungen mit Zeitgenossen*. Weimar: Hermann Böhlaus Nachfolger, 1930. 200 pp.

Contains a letter written by Amadeus Wendt to Tieck in March 1823, a letter from Tieck to August Klingemann dated 24 June 1823, and Klingemann's reply from 8 September 1823. All letters focus on Christian Dietrich Grabbe and are accompanied by brief commentary.

539. ___, ed. *Christian Dietrich Grabbe. Werke und Briefe: Historisch-kritische Gesamtausgabe in sechs Bänden*, Vol. 1. Emsdetten (Westf.): Lechte, 1960. xv + 676 pp.

Includes Tieck's famous letter to Grabbe from 6 December 1822, in which he judges the emerging author's *Gothland* as well as his overall talent as an author.

540. Campe, Elisabeth, ed. *Aus dem Leben von Johann Diederich Gries: Nach seinen eigenen und den Briefen*

*seiner Zeitgenossen.* Leipzig: F.A. Brockhaus, 1855. 198 pp.

A letter from Tieck to the translator Gries dated 28 April 1828 is printed on p. 148.

541. Cohn, Alfons Fedor, ed. *Wilhelm von Burgsdorff: Briefe an Brinkman, Henriette von Finckenstein, Wilhelm v. Humboldt, Rahel, Friedrich Tieck, Ludwig Tieck und Wiesel.* Deutsche Literaturdenkmale des 18. und 19. Jahrhunderts, Vol. 139. Berlin: B. Behr, 1907. xv + 230 pp.

Pp. 166-176 present a lengthy letter from Burgsdorff to Tieck dated 15 May 1799. The topic is contemporary French theater.

542. Fiebiger, Otto. "Ein Brief Ludwig Tiecks an Carl Gustav von Brinkman." *Euphorion*, Supplemental Vol. 13 (1921): 61-74.

A letter to the Swedish diplomat dated 17 November 1835.

543. Fritze, Franz, trans. *Sämmtliche Tragödien des Sophokles: Metrisch übertragen.* Berlin: A. Förstner, 1845. xxiv + 521 pp.

As an introduction to this volume, Fritze includes a letter addressed to him by Tieck in 1843. Dealing with the metrical qualities of Fritze's *Electra* translation, this letter was republished by Tieck as "Ein Brief an den Uebersetzer der Elektra: 1843" on pp. 419-424 of his *Kritische Schriften*, Vol. 2. Leipzig: F.A. Brockhaus, 1848. vi + 424 pp.

544. Hoffmann von Fallersleben, August Heinrich. *Findlinge: Zur Geschichte deutscher Sprache und Dichtung.* Leipzig: Engelmann, 1860. viii + 496 pp.

Includes, on p. 149, a letter from Tieck to Riemer dated 3 July 1841.

545. Houben, H.H., ed. *Damals in Weimar: Erinnerungen und Briefe von und an Johanna Schopenhauer*. Leipzig: Klinkhardt & Biermann, 1924. viii + 358 pp.

Pp. 260-262 contain a letter from Tieck to Johanna Schopenhauer postmarked 2 May 1824.

546. Meisner, Heinrich and Erich Schmidt, eds. *Briefe an Wolfgang Menzel*. Mitteilungen aus dem Litteraturarchive in Berlin. Berlin: Litteraturarchiv-Gesellschaft, 1908. xiv + 295 pp.

Six letters from Tieck to Menzel, dated 1828-1841, are printed on pp. 263-273.

547. ___, eds. *Briefe an Rudolf Köpke*. Mitteilungen aus dem Litteraturarchive in Berlin, N.S., Vol. 1. Berlin: Litteraturarchiv-Gesellschaft, 1909. 84 pp.

Contains one letter from Tieck, which Köpke received on 29 March 1853 (see pp. 83 ff.).

548. Schemann, Ludwig, ed. *Einiges aus dem Reuss'schen Briefwechsel*. Göttingen: Dieterich, 1888. 27 pp.

P. 27 holds a letter from Tieck to the Göttingen Professor Jeremias David Reuss dated 28 June 1819.

549. *Unveröffentlichte Briefe: Ludwig Tieck an Theodor von Küstner. Albert Niemann an Botho von Hülsen*. (Den Besuchern des Staatstheater Museums: Der General-Intendant der Preußischen Staatstheater). Berlin: n.p., 1930. 5 pp.

A letter from Tieck to a Berlin theater director. This publication is apparently only available at the Deutsche Staatsbibliothek, Berlin, under "Briefe, unveröffentlichte," call no. Yz 12097/50.

550. Zoeppritz, Rudolf, ed. *Aus F.H. Jacobis Nachlaß: Ungedruckte Briefe von und an Jacobi und Andere. Nebst ungedruckten Gedichten von Goethe und Lenz*, Vol. 2. Leipzig: Engelmann, 1869. viii + 325 pp.

Contains, on p. 32, a letter from Tieck to Jacobi written around 1808.

Cross ref.: 48 (König Friedrich Wilhelm IV. von Preußen, A. von Humboldt, Illaire, Müller, Willisen, Graf York-Wartenburg), 587 and 634 (von der Hagen).

*ii.* Unknown Correspondents

551. Retland, J. Florus [J. Tandler]. "Ein Brief von Ludwig Tieck." *Hausblätter*, 1862, Vol. 1, pp. 77-80.

An unaddressed letter dated 31 December 1832, in which Tieck recommends the work of an unnamed author. The recipient of the letter may well have been a publisher.

552. ___. "Ein zweiter Brief von Ludwig Tieck." *Hausblätter*, 1862, Vol. 2, pp. 77-80.

An unaddressed letter dated 20 December 1807. Tieck requests its recipient to procure a book for him.

Cross ref.: 48, 606.

# VIII. Tieck as Critic

## 1. GENERAL

553. Gries, Frauke. "Ludwig Tieck as Critic: Sociological Tendencies in his Criticism." Diss. Stanford, 1967. Abstract in *DAI*, 28, No. 07A (1968): 2645.

   Surveys Tieck's *Kritische Schriften*, examines their "relationship to contemporary methods of literary criticism," and concludes that they display a "disposition toward a sociological approach to literature."

554. Hettner, Hermann. "Ludwig Tieck als Kritiker." *Blätter für literarische Unterhaltung*, 16 (1853): 361-363. Reprinted pp. 354-358 in Hettner, *Schriften zur Literatur*, ed. Jürgen Jahn. Berlin: Aufbau-Verlag, 1959. xlvi + 390 pp.

   A favorable, albeit superficial, review of Tieck's *Kritische Schriften*.

555. Hewett-Thayer, Harvey W. "Tieck's Marginalia in the British Museum." *GR*, 9 (1934): 9-17.

   Studies Tieck's notes as found in a wide variety of books located at the British Museum, including many volumes on

English and Spanish literature. This discussion is continued in no. 571. See also nos. 568 and 574.

556. Paulin, Roger. "Ludwig Tiecks Essayistik." *JIG*, 14, No. 1 (1982): 126-156.

An informative overview of Tieck's numerous essays on language, literature, and art, many of which prefaced works he edited. Includes an extensive bibliography of Tieck's critical writings.

557. Wellek, René. *A History of Modern Criticism: 1750-1950*, Vol. 2: *The Romantic Age*. New Haven, London: Yale University Press, 1955. v + 459 pp.

This renowned work contains, on pp. 93-100, a quick survey of Tieck's critical writings that, unfortunately, ends on a sour note, with the observation that "not much in the way of theory can be learned from Tieck."

Cross ref.: 57.

## 2. DRAMA CRITICISM, STAGE REFORMS, WORK AS "DRAMATURG"

### a. General

558. Bastier, Paul. "Le paradoxe sur le comédien: Talma, Tieck et Roetscher pour et contre Diderot." *RLC*, 12 (1932): 871-875.

With reference to Tieck, only an inconclusive note concerning his views on acting.

559. Bischoff, Heinrich. *Ludwig Tieck als Dramaturg*. Bibliothèque de la Faculté de Philosophie et Lettres de l'Uni-

versité de Liége, Vol. 2. Brussels: Office de Publicité, Société Belge de Librairie, 1897. 124 pp.

This careful analysis of Tieck's writings on dramatic theory as well as on the theaters of England, Spain, France, Italy, and Germany comes to the conclusion that Tieck has been underrated both as drama critic and theater producer.

560. Drach, Erich. *Ludwig Tiecks Bühnenreformen*. Berlin: R. Trenkel, 1909. 92 pp.

An outdated summary of Tieck's stage reforms that has largely been superseded by no. 563. Details concerning individual productions incorporating these reforms are found in nos. 566, 570, 572, 577, and 579.

561. Gross, Edgar. "Der unsterbliche Tieck: Zu seinem 100. Todestag am 28. April." *Neue literarische Welt*, 4, No. 8 (1953): 9.

Note on Tieck's activities as "Dramaturg" and on his importance for the modern stage.

562. Günther, Johannes. "Das Drama in den Theaterkritiken des Romantikers Ludwig Tieck." *Der Zwinger: Zeitschrift für Weltanschauung, Theater und Kunst, Dresden*, 5 (1921): 177-181.

Pieces together Tieck's views on drama and the stage via a study of his critical essays.

563. Kemme, Hans-Martin. "Ludwig Tiecks Bühnenreformpläne und -versuche und ihre Wirkung auf die Entwicklung des deutschen Theaters im 19. und 20. Jahrhundert." Diss. Berlin, 1971.

A much-needed update of no. 560 that adds valuable information regarding the reception of Tieck's stage reforms. See nos. 566, 570, 572, 577, and 579 for discussions of individual stage performances showcasing Tieck's numerous reforms.

564. Schwarzlose, Walter. "Methoden der deutschen Theaterkritik untersucht an den Kritiken von Lessing, Tieck, Laube, Rötscher, Fontane, Kerr." Diss. Münster, 1951.

Emphasizes the practical aspects of Tieck's drama criticism.

565. Weissert, Otto. *Ludwig Tieck als Kritiker des Dramas und Theaters*. Darmstadt: Roetherdruck, 1928. 75 pp.

Tieck's achievements as drama critic are placed into the context of "Geistesgeschichte."

Cross ref.: 173, 260, 709, 713.

### b. Concerning Jonson, Shakespeare, the Elizabethan Drama

566. Asper, Helmut G. "Ludwig Tieck inszeniert *Was ihr Wollt*: Beschreibung und Analyse einer Fiktion." *JDSh*, 110 (1974): 134-147.

Actual stage reforms undertaken by Tieck in the course of his Dresden and Berlin Shakespeare productions (see nos. 570, 572, and 577) were largely foreshadowed by a fictional account of an *As You Like it* staging in his novella "Der junge Tischlermeister."

567. Delius, N. *Die Tieck'sche Shaksperekritik*. Bonn: H.B. König, 1846. xvi + 182 pp. Reprinted Hildesheim, New York: Georg Olms, 1981.

Designed as a supplement to the Schlegel-Tieck translations of Shakespeare's dramatic works, this volume summarizes Tieck's critical commentary, as derived from a variety of sources, on each of the translated plays. Tieck's comments range in topic from the dating of Shakespeare's works to the problems inherent in their translation.

568. Fischer, Walther. "Zu Ludwig Tiecks elizabethanischen Studien: Tieck als Ben Jonson-Philologe." *JDSh*, 62 (1926): 98-131.

Summarizes Tieck's extensive research on Jonson as well as the marginalia found in his personal Jonson editions. For more on Tieck's marginalia, see nos. 555, 571, and 574.

569. Fiumi, Annamaria Borsano. *La critica Shakespeariana di Ludwig Tieck*. Milan, Varese: Instituto editoriale cisalpino, 1970. 191 pp.

Essentially an Italian version of no. 576.

570. Grünbaum, Anita. "Von Tiecks *Sommernachtstraum*-Inszenierung zur ersten Aufführung in Stockholm." *Kleine Schriften der Gesellschaft für Theatergeschichte*, 20 (1964): 36-58.

Tieck's dramatic innovations, as showcased in his 1843 production of *A Midsummer Night's Dream* (no. 577), formed the basis of a Swedish staging of this Shakespeare play in 1860.

571. Hewett-Thayer, Harvey W. "Tieck and the Elizabethan Drama: His Marginalia." *JEGP*, 34 (1935): 377-407.

A continuation of no. 555, this time with particular emphasis on Tieck's marginalia in his editions of Ben Jonson and in works dealing with the Elizabethan period. See also nos. 568 and 574.

572. Hille, Gertrud. "Die Tieck-Semperische Rekonstruktion des Fortuna-Theaters: Ein Beitrag zur Geschichte der Bühnenreformen im 19. Jahrhundert." *Schriften der Gesellschaft für Theatergeschichte*, 39 (1929): 72-109.

Tieck based the design of his new Shakespeare stage on a British model dating back to 1600. Hille's article examines several German Shakespeare productions using this design.

573. Joachimi-Dege, Marie. *Deutsche Shakespeare-Probleme im XVIII. Jahrhundert und im Zeitalter der Romantik*. Untersuchungen zur neueren Sprach- und Literaturgeschichte, Vol. 12. Leipzig: H. Haessel, 1907. 296 pp.

A survey of eighteenth and nineteenth century German Shakespeare criticism showing particularly how the Schlegels and Tieck took steps to revise the criticism put forth by their predecessors during the Age of Enlightenment as well as during the Storm and Stress and Classical periods.

574. Kerber, Erich. "Neues über Ludwig Tiecks Shakespeare-Studien." *Bühne und Welt*, 15, No. 2 (1913): 62-67.

Comments on the marginalia found in Tieck's personal Shakespeare editions. For more on marginalia, see nos. 555, 568, and 571.

575. Koch, Max. "Ludwig Tieck's Stellung zu Shakespeare: Einleitender Vortrag zur Jahresversammlung der deutschen Shakespeare-Gesellschaft am 23. April 1896." *JDSh*, 32 (1896): 330-347.

Claims that Tieck understood Shakespeare better than any of his contemporaries and celebrates him as the initiator of German Shakespearean scholarship.

576. Lüdeke, H. *Ludwig Tieck und das alte englische Theater: Ein Beitrag zur Geschichte der Romantik*. Deutsche Forschungen, Vol. 6. Frankfurt am Main: Moritz Diesterweg, 1922. viii + 373 pp.

The best, most comprehensive treatment of Tieck's lifelong interest in Shakespeare as well as in the Elizabethan drama in general. Includes a historical sketch of German Shakespeare criticism prior to Tieck, information on Tieck's

Shakespeare translations, and a discussion of the "Dichterleben" novellas, which have Shakespeare as their subject.

577. Petersen, Julius. "Ludwig Tiecks Sommernachtstraum-Inszenierung." *Neues Archiv für Theatergeschichte*, 1 (1930): 163-198.

A thorough analysis of Tieck's *A Midsummer Night's Dream* production (Berlin, 1843) focusing primarily on his abandonment of sliding scene technology in favor of a simpler, more abstract multilevel stage arrangement popular in Germany until the advent of the revolving stage (see also no. 570).

578. Prölss, Robert. "Shakespeare-Aufführungen in Dresden vom 20. Oct. 1816 bis Ende 1860." *JDSh*, 15 (1880): 173-210.

Much of this article is devoted to Tieck who, as "Dramaturg" at the Dresden theater from 1820-1842, greatly increased the theater's Shakespeare repertoire and, in addition, replaced the old Shakespeare translations with the vastly superior "Schlegel-Tieck."

Cross ref.: 374, 375, 385.

### c. Other

579. Brandt, Heinrich. *Goethes Faust auf der Kgl. sächsischen Hofbühne zu Dresden: Ein Beitrag zur Theaterwissenschaft*. Germanische Studien, Vol. 8. Berlin: E. Ebering, 1921. xvi + 274 pp.

A detailed history of the Dresden *Faust* productions which, from 1820-1842, were greatly influenced by Tieck's dramatic theories.

580. Kummer, Friedrich. "Vom Schicksal der *Dame Kobold*." *Die Bühne*, Berlin, 20 May 1939, pp. 244-245.

On Tieck's unsuccessful Calderón productions in Dresden in 1826.

## 3. MISCELLANEOUS

581. Gries, Frauke. "Eine unbeachtet gebliebene Rezension von Ludwig Tieck: 'Belisar, Trauerspiel in fünf Akten von Ed. v. Schenk.'" *ZDP*, 90 (1971): 191-199.

Discusses a review by Tieck that was neither completed nor published due to flaws in argumentation and style.

582. ___. "Two Critical Essays by Ludwig Tieck: On Literature and its Sociological Aspects." *Monatshefte*, 66 (1974): 157-165.

Introduction to a pair of essays written by Tieck in 1828 entitled "Kritik und deutsches Bücherwesen" and "Goethe und seine Zeit." The first prefaces a new edition of Schnabel's *Insel Felsenburg*; the second introduces Tieck's edition of Lenz's collected works.

583. Rüter, Hubert. "Eine Horen-Rezension Ludwig Tiecks." *ZDP*, 95 (1976): 204-211.

Tieck authored the negative review of Goethe's Cellini translation appearing in the journal *Deutschland* in 1796.

584. Scholte, J.H. "Die Romantik und Grimmelshausen." *GRM*, 34 (1953): 190-200.

Credits Tieck with having initiated German Grimmelshausen scholarship via his appreciation of the original (unadulterated) edition of *Simplicissimus Teutsch* (1669).

# IX. Tieck as Editor and Translator

## 1. EDITORIAL WORK

### a. Medieval German Literature

585. Brinker-Gabler, Gisela. "Wissenschaftlich-poetische Mittelalterrezeption in der Romantik." Pp. 80-97 in *Romantik: Ein literaturwissenschaftliches Studienbuch*, ed. Ernst Ribbat. Athenäum-Taschenbücher, Vol. 2149. Königstein/Ts.: Athenäum, 1979. 236 pp.

   As far as Tieck is concerned, a prelude to the next item.

586. ___.*Poetisch-wissenschaftliche Mittelalterrezeption: Ludwig Tiecks Erneuerung altdeutscher Literatur*. Göppinger Arbeiten zur Germanistik, Vol. 309. Göppingen: Kümmerle, 1980. 299 pp.

   A detailed examination of the function, development, and reception of Tieck's various editions of medieval German literature. Valuable.

587. Klee, Gotthold. *Zu Ludwig Tiecks germanistischen Studien*. Programm Bautzen, Vol. 543. Bautzen: E.M. Monse, 1895. 31 pp.

This overview is devoted primarily to Tieck's editions of medieval works, although his *Deutsches Theater*, focusing on later literature, is also considered. Includes the following previously unpublished correspondence, all having to do with Tieck's various editorial projects: two letters from Tieck to A.W. Schlegel dated September 1802 and 30 May 1803 respectively, one letter from Tieck to von der Hagen dated 24 December 1810, and one letter from Tieck to the publisher Mohr in Heidelberg written on 28 September 1816.

588. Körner, Josef. *Nibelungenforschungen der deutschen Romantik*. Untersuchungen zur neueren Sprach- und Literatur-Geschichte, N.S., Vol. 9. Leipzig: H. Haessel, 1911. viii + 273 pp. Reprinted Darmstadt: Wissenschaftliche Buchgesellschaft, 1968.

Tieck's work on an edition of the *Nibelungenlied* is discussed on pp. 55 ff. The unfinished project is today part of Tieck's literary remains. For more on this subject, see nos. 585 and 586.

589. Meves, Uwe. "Zu Ludwig Tiecks poetologischem Konzept bei der Erneuerung mittelhochdeutscher Dichtungen." Pp. 107-126 in *Mittelalter-Rezeption: Gesammelte Vorträge des Salzburger Symposions "Die Rezeption mittelalterlicher Dichter und ihrer Werke in Literatur, bildender Kunst und Musik des 19. und 20. Jahrhunderts,"* ed. Jürgen Kühnel, Hans-Dieter Mück, and Ulrich Müller. Göppinger Arbeiten zur Germanistik, Vol. 286. Göppingen: Kümmerle, 1979. 631 pp.

It was Tieck's intent in his editions of medieval German literature to present – by way of a reminder of Germany's great "romantic" past – an antidote to modern society, industrialization, and especially to emerging capitalism and consumerism.

## b. German Renaissance and Baroque Literature

590. Kiesant, Knut. "Zur Rezeption der Literatur des 17. Jahrhunderts durch die Romantik." *WB*, 26, No. 12 (1980): 36-48.

    Pp. 42-45 of this article constitute a Marxist interpretation of Tieck's commentary on Baroque literature in his *Deutsches Theater* of 1817.

591. Krohn, Rüdiger. "Die Rückkehr des Bürgerpoeten: Aspekte der Hans-Sachs-Rezeption in der literarischen Frühromantik." Pp. 80-106 in *Mittelalter-Rezeption: Gesammelte Vorträge des Salzburger Symposions "Die Rezeption mittelalterlicher Dichter und ihrer Werke in Literatur, bildender Kunst und Musik des 19. und 20. Jahrhunderts,"* ed. Jürgen Kühnel, Hans-Dieter Mück, and Ulrich Müller. Göppinger Arbeiten zur Germanistik, Vol. 286. Göppingen: Kümmerle, 1979. 631 pp.

    Pp. 95 ff. contain notes on Tieck's critical reception of Sachs, especially as it manifests itself in *Deutsches Theater*.

592. Paulin, Roger. "Tieck's *Deutsches Theater* (1817) and its Significance." Pp. 569-577 in *From Wolfram and Petrarch to Goethe and Grass: Studies in Literature in Honour of Leonard Forster*, ed. D.H. Green, L.P. Johnson, and Dieter Wuttke. Saecula spiritalia, Vol. 5. Baden-Baden: Valentin Koerner, 1982. 642 pp.

    Portrays Tieck, via his editorial work in *Deutsches Theater*, as a major contributor to the rediscovery of German Renaissance and Baroque literature.

593. Riederer, Frank. *Ludwig Tiecks Beziehungen zur deutschen Literatur des 17. Jahrhunderts*. Greifswald: Julius Abel, 1915. 125 pp.

Credits Tieck with having done much to popularize German Baroque literature in nineteenth century Germany through his editorial projects (particularly *Deutsches Theater*), but attacks him for not having assimilated it into his own literary works to the extent that Arnim and Brentano did.

Cross ref.: 587.

### c. Schnabel's *Insel Felsenburg*, Lenz and Kleist Editions

594. Freye, Karl. "Die Lenz-Ausgabe Ludwig Tiecks." *Zeitschrift für Bücherfreunde*, N.S. 4 (1913): 247-249.

Points out errors in Tieck's 1828 edition of J.M.R. Lenz's collected works. Includes a newly found letter from Tieck to the publisher Reimer dated 16 July 1828 (a further letter concerning this project is printed in no. 528).

595. Kanzog, Klaus. *Edition und Engagement: 150 Jahre Editionsgeschichte der Werke und Briefe Heinrich von Kleists*. Quellen und Forschungen zur Sprach- und Kulturgeschichte der germanischen Völker, N.S., Vols. 74 and 75. Berlin, New York: Walter de Gruyter, 1979. 342, 388 pp.

Vol. 1 (pp. 74-132) contains a detailed discussion on Tieck's views concerning Kleist and his oeuvre, his reasons for publishing Kleist's works, his editorial policy, and the reception of his Kleist editions of 1821 and 1826. Vol. 2 contains various documentary materials pertaining to these editions. See also no. 527.

596. Köhler, Reinhold. *Zu Heinrich von Kleist's Werken: Die Lesarten der Originalausgaben und die Aenderungen Ludwig Tieck's und Julian Schmidt's*. Weimar: Hermann Böhlau, 1862. viii + 108 pp.

An editorial history of Kleist's oeuvre, with much emphasis on the efforts of Tieck. No. 527 should also be considered in this context.

597. Stern, Martin. "Die wunderlichen Fata der 'Insel Felsenburg': Tiecks Anteil an der Neuausgabe von J.G. Schnabels Roman (1828). Eine Richtigstellung." *DVLG*, 40 (1966): 109-115.

Stern contends that Tieck wrote the introduction to the 1828 edition of Schnabel's *Insel Felsenburg*, but was not responsible for revisions made to the text.

Cross ref.: 582.

**d. Other**

598. Wetzel, Johannes Volkmar. *Adelheid Reinbold, die Schülerin Tiecks*. Leipzig: A. Hoffmann, 1911. 65 pp.

On the minor Dresden writer Adelheid Reinbold (aka Franz Berthold), several of whose works Tieck edited and supplied with introductions.

## 2. TRANSLATIONS

**a. From the English**

*i.* General

599. Zeydel, Edwin H. "Ludwig Tieck as a Translator of English." *PMLA*, 51 (1936): 221-242.

Lists chronologically and discusses all translations from the English which Tieck undertook or in which he had a share.

*ii*. Shakespeare

600. Bernays, Michael. "Der Schlegel-Tieck'sche Shakespeare." *JDSh*, 1 (1865): 396-405.

   A general introduction to the content and genesis of the "Schlegel-Tieck" Shakespeare translations.

601. Flatter, Richard. "Schlegel und 'Schlegel-Tieck.'" Pp. 70-83 in Flatter, *Triumph der Gnade: Shakespeare Essays*. Vienna, Munich, Basel: Kurt Desch, 1956. 175 pp.

   Argues that A.W. Schlegel and Tieck never worked on the Shakespeare translations together and that Schlegel incorporated none of Tieck's suggestions into the 17 pieces he contributed to the collection later completed by Dorothea Tieck and Graf Wolf Baudissin.

602. Jost, Walter. "Stilkrise der deutschen Shakespeare-Übersetzung." *DVLG*, 35 (1961): 1-43.

   As German Shakespeare translations go, the "Schlegel-Tieck" has yet to be surpassed. Its strengths lie in the areas of style, expression, and feeling for the English language.

603. Kahn, Ludwig W. "Ludwig Tieck als Übersetzer von Shakespeares Sonetten." *GR*, 9 (1934): 140-142.

   Despite plans to translate all of Shakespeare's sonnets, Tieck managed to complete but a handful, and then only as rough drafts. Two such drafts are printed here for the first time.

604. Langermann, H. von. "Ein Brief des Grafen Wolf Baudissin über die Vollendung der Schlegel-Tieckschen Shakespeare-Übersetzung." *JDSh*, 71 (1935): 107-109.

   In his letter, Baudissin praises Tieck's extensive knowledge of sixteenth and seventeenth century drama as well as his helpful comments regarding the translation of Shakespeare.

605. Larson, Kenneth E. "The Origins of the 'Schlegel-Tieck' Shakespeare in the 1820s." *GQ*, 60 (1987): 19-37.

Significant interest in German Shakespeare translations prompted the publisher Reimer to engage the services of Tieck, and through him, of his daughter Dorothea and of Graf Wolf Baudissin to complete the series of Shakespeare translations begun earlier by A.W. Schlegel (compare no. 607). Concerning the interactions between Tieck and Schlegel, see no. 601.

606. Lüdeke, H. "Zur Tieck'schen Shakespeare-Übersetzung." *JDSh*, 55 (1919): 1-29.

On Tieck's incomplete translation of *Love's Labour's Lost* dating from the period 1800-1809, which was later revised and brought to a close by Baudissin. Includes two previously unpublished Tieck letters concerning the translation of Shakespeare, the first written to A.W. Schlegel in 1825 and the second directed to an unknown correspondent in 1829.

607. Schulz, W. "Der Anteil des Grafen Wolf Baudissin an der Shakespeareübersetzung Schlegel-Tiecks." *ZDP*, 59 (1934): 52-67.

Based on his diary entries, it appears that Baudissin was a driving force behind the completion of the "Schlegel-Tieck" Shakespeare translations, to which he devoted much time as editor and proofreader. See also nos. 604-606 for more on Baudissin's involvement in the project.

Cross ref.: 567.

### iii. Sheridan

608. Trainer, James. "Tieck's Translation of *The Rivals.*" *MLQ*, 21 (1960): 246-252.

    A stylistic analysis of Tieck's unpublished Sheridan translation of 1850.

### iv. Other

609. Littlejohns, Richard. "Ludwig Tieck und drei 'englische Moderomane': Geschichte und Klärung einiger Mißverständnisse." *Archiv*, 217 (1980): 32-38.

    Provides additional information concerning a problem already dealt with by Maassen (see next item).

610. Maassen, Carl Georg von. "Übersetzungen englischer Romane, die fälschlich Ludwig Tieck zugeschrieben wurden (Berichtigungen zu Holzmann-Bohatta, Goedeke und Hayn)." *Der grundgescheute Antiquarius*, 1 (1920/22): 157-159.

    Discusses three translations from the English wrongly attributed to Tieck by Carl August Nicolai (see also preceding item).

Cross ref.: 178 (Jonson).

## b. From Middle High German

611. Brüggemann, Joseph. *Ludwig Tieck als Übersetzer mittelhochdeutscher Dichtung: Eine Kritik*. Trier: Jacob Lintz, 1908. 63 pp.

    Praises Tieck's translations of MHG texts less for their technical or artistic virtuosity than for the fact that they, in their time, served as important models for the emerging discipline of Germanic philology.

## c. From the Spanish

### i. Cervantes

612. Branky, Franz. "Welch und Welches in Tiecks Don Quijote-Übersetzung." *Zeitschrift für den deutschen Unterricht*, 9 (1895): 768-770.

    Trivial study of grammatical inconsistencies.

613. König, Bernhard. "Der irrende Ritter und sein Stallmeister: Zwei Anmerkungen zu Tiecks Übersetzung des *Don Quijote*." *Romanistisches Jahrbuch*, 12 (1961): 343-351.

    Uncovers errors in Tieck's translation.

614. Kronacher, Bettina. *Bertuchs Don Quijote-Übersetzung unter Einbeziehung der ihm nächstfolgenden Übersetzungen von Tieck und Soltau*. [Germany]: n.p., n.d. 2pp. Excerpt of Diss. Munich, 1924.

    Tieck's translation of *Don Quixote* (1799) is much more faithful to the Spanish original that that of F.J. Bertuch (1775), which is heavily criticized in the present work.

### ii. Espinel

615. Jacobs, Jürgen. "Der Picaro im bürgerlichen Zeitalter: Zu Ludwig Tiecks Übersetzung des *Marcos de Obregón* und zu seiner Novelle *Wunderlichkeiten*." *Arcadia: Zeitschrift für vergleichende Literaturwissenschaft*, 24 (1989): 263-270.

    Probes Tieck's reasons for translating Vincente Espinel's picaresque novel at a time (1827) when the genre was unpopular in Germany due to its negative moral and social implications. Also analyzes Tieck's "Wunderlichkeiten" (1837), in which the picaresque tradition is discussed.

# X. Tieck and Art, Music, Education, Philosophy, Politics, and Religion

## 1. ART

### a. General

616. Bosch, Eva. "Dichtung über Kunst bei Ludwig Tieck." Diss. Munich, 1962.

    A broad survey of works by Tieck containing references to art, artists, and the process of artistic creation.

617. Cullmann, Rudolf. "Tiecks Kunstbetrachtung im Zusammenhang mit seiner Persönlichkeit und seiner Dichtung." Diss. Freiburg i.B., 1921. Abstract in *Jahreshefte der Universität Freiburg i.B.*, 5 (1920/21): 13-17.

    Traces the development of Tieck's views on art, particularly with reference to the criteria "Verstand" and "Phantasie." Argues that these views were not molded by Wackenroder to the degree assumed by many critics.

618. Hartmann, Hans. *Kunst und Religion bei Wackenroder, Tieck und Solger*. Solingen: Alb. Pfeiffer, 1916. iv + 63 pp.

Superficial overview not up to modern critical standards.

619. Strack, Friedrich. "Die 'göttliche' Kunst und ihre Sprache: Zum Kunst- und Religionsbegriff bei Wackenroder, Tieck und Novalis." Pp. 369-391 in *Romantik in Deutschland: Ein interdisziplinäres Symposium*, ed. Richard Brinkmann. *DVLG* Sonderband. Stuttgart: J.B. Metzler, 1978. x + 722 pp.

Art, as presented in Tieck's various earlier works, is no longer in the service of religion, as it was for Wackenroder or Novalis, but instead expresses the purely aesthetic and sensual.

Cross ref.: 430-432, 434, 436-438, 441, 445, 447, 448, 657, 703.

**b. Tieck and Runge**

620. Aubert, Andreas. *Runge und die Romantik*. Berlin: Paul Cassirer, 1909. 127 pp.

Much of this profusely illustrated monograph is devoted to the close friendship between Tieck and Runge. Although numerous sections deal with Tieck's influence on Runge, more critical discussions of this topic can be found in the following items.

621. Feilchenfeldt, Konrad. "Runge und die Dichter." *JDSG*, 21 (1977): 297-326.

Pp. 304-311 deal with the influence of Tieck's *Sternbald* on Runge's *Hinterlassene Schriften* (1840/41).

622. Franke, Christa. *Philipp Otto Runge und die Kunstansichten Wackenroders und Tiecks*. Marburger Beiträge

zur Germanistik, Vol. 49. Marburg: N.G. Elwert, 1974. 137 pp.

The most informative study available concerning Tieck's influence on Runge's art. Updates nos. 620, 623, and 624.

623. Grundy, J.B.C. *Tieck and Runge: A Study in the Relationship of Literature and Art in the Romantic Period with Especial Reference to "Franz Sternbald."* Studien zur deutschen Kunstgeschichte, Vol. 270. Strassburg: J.H.Ed. Heitz, 1930. 110 pp.

A forerunner of the preceding item, this monograph demonstrates that Runge's perceptions of landscape and color were heavily indebted to Tieck, particularly to *Sternbald*.

624. Krebs, Siegfried. *Philipp Otto Runges Entwicklung unter dem Einflusse Ludwig Tiecks: Mit 5 ungedruckten Briefen Tiecks.* Beiträge zur neueren Literaturgeschichte, Vol. 1, No. 4. Heidelberg: Winter, 1909. 168 pp.

Less a study of Tieck's influence on Runge than of the latter's reception of Jakob Böhme, to whose mysticism he was introduced by Tieck. Contains five previously unpublished letters from Tieck to his sister Sophie, which are largely irrelevant to the topic at hand.

625. Nabbe, Hildegard. "Die geheime Schrift der Natur: Ludwig Tiecks und Philipp Otto Runges Auffassung der Hieroglyphe." *Seminar*, 25 (1989): 12-36.

On the differences of opinion between Runge and Tieck vis-à-vis the importance of hieroglyphic images for romantic art.

c. **Tieck, Wackenroder, and their Collaborative Projects** *Herzensergießungen eines Kunstliebenden Klosterbruders* **(1797) and** *Phantasien über die Kunst* **(1799)**

626. Alewyn, Richard. "Wackenroders Anteil." *GR*, 19 (1944): 48-58.

    Clarifies misconceptions concerning the true authorship of various parts of *Herzensergießungen* and *Phantasien* (see also no. 628).

627. Gladow, Gudrun. "Größe und Gefahr der Wackenroder-Tieckschen Kunstanschauung." *Zeitschrift für deutsche Bildung*, 14 (1938): 162-169.

    A discussion of romantic aesthetics as expressed primarily in *Herzensergießungen*.

628. Kohlschmidt, Werner. "Bemerkungen zu Wackenroders und Tiecks Anteil an den *Phantasien über die Kunst.*" Pp. 89-99 in *Philologia Deutsch: Festschrift zum 70. Geburtstag von Walter Henzen*, ed. Werner Kohlschmidt and Paul Zinsli. Berne: Francke, 1965. 167 pp.

    Attempts to prove that Tieck contributed more to *Phantasien* than previously anticipated (especially by Alewyn in no. 626).

629. ___. "Der junge Tieck und Wackenroder." Pp. 30-44 in *Die deutsche Romantik: Poetik, Formen und Motive*, ed. Hans Steffen. Kleine Vandenhoeck-Reihe, Vol. 250. Göttingen: Vandenhoeck & Ruprecht, 1967. 288 pp.

    General commentary on the friendship between Tieck and Wackenroder, their views on art, and especially their collaborative projects.

630. Lippuner, Heinz. *Wackenroder/Tieck und die bildende Kunst.* Zurich: Juris, 1965. viii + 225 pp.

Portrays the literary collaboration between Tieck and Wackenroder as "der Beginn der romantischen Aesthetik." Contains a useful look at how the two men perceived the artistic traditions of France, Germany, Italy, and the Netherlands.

631. Santoli, Vittorio. "L. Tieck e W.H. Wackenroder (a proposito del concetto dell'arte)." *La Cultura: Rivista mensile di filosofia, lettere, arte*, 5 (1925/26): 63-68.

The world of art, as presented in *Herzensergießungen* and *Phantasien*, is typically romantic in that it expresses man's longing for the eternal.

632. Wiedemann-Lambinus, Margarete. "Die romantische Kunstanschauung Wackenroders und Tiecks." *Zeitschrift für Ästhetik und allgemeine Kunstwissenschaft*, 32 (1938): 26-45.

Via their collaborative projects, Tieck and Wackenroder rediscovered the Middle Ages for German literature, art, and music.

Cross ref.: 447, 617, 635, 642-644.


### d. Other

633. Danton, George Henry. *Tieck's Essay on the Boydell Shakspere Gallery*. Ottendorfer Memorial Series of Germanic Monographs, Vol. 3. Indianapolis: Edward J. Hecker, 1912. 50 pp.

Summarizes Tieck's negative art review "Die Kupferstiche nach der Shakespeare-Gallerie in London" (1793). Little in the way of critical commentary on Danton's part. Annoying orthography.

634. Grunewald, Eckhard. "Die 'Heldenbilder' der Brüder Tieck: Mit zwei unveröffentlichten Briefen Ludwig Tiecks und Friedrich von der Hagens." *Aurora*, 43 (1983): 134-150.

Provides the historical background for the 1819 publication of Ludwig and Friedrich Tieck's lithograph collection depicting famous medieval heroes. Includes unpublished Tieck-von der Hagen correspondence from the years 1818-1819 as well as numerous illustrations.

635. Littlejohns, Richard. "Die Madonna von Pommersfelden: Geschichte einer romantischen Begeisterung." *Aurora*, 45 (1985): 163-188.

The reactions of Tieck and Wackenroder to a painting attributed to Cornelis van Cleve, which the two viewed on their journey from Erlangen to Göttingen in 1793.

636. Nabbe, Hildegard. "Ludwig Tieck: Eine Studie zu seinen späteren Äußerungen über bildende Kunst und ihre Randgebiete." Diss. Toronto, 1974. Abstract in *DAI*, 37, No. 12A (1977): 7774.

A study of Tieck's notes on art history as preserved in his unpublished manuscript "Geschichte und Theorie der bildenden Künste" located in Vienna.

637. ___. "Ludwig Tiecks Verhältnis zu Correggio." *Seminar*, 13 (1977): 154-169.

Examines Tieck's opinions concerning artwork by Correggio as well as a drama centering on this Italian painter's life written by the Danish romanticist Oehlenschläger.

638. Paulin, Roger. "Tiecks Empfindungen vor Caspar David Friedrichs Landschaft." *Aurora*, 43 (1983): 151-159.

On Tieck's perceptions regarding Friedrich's landscapes.

Cross ref.: 686.

## 2. MUSIC

639. Atkinson, Margaret E. "Musical Form in Some Romantic Writings." *MLR*, 44 (1949): 218-227.

    Tieck's works, like those of Wackenroder and Brentano, exhibit "musical rather than literary composition." Superseded by no. 644.

640. Bolte, Johannes. "Aus einer Anekdotensammlung Ludwig Tiecks." Pp. 22-25 in *Festschrift Hermann Kretzschmar zum 70. Geburtstage überreicht von Kollegen, Schülern und Freunden*. Leipzig: C.F. Peters, 1918. vi + 184 pp. Reprinted Hildesheim, New York: Georg Olms, 1973.

    A selection of anecdotes on the subject of music stemming from Tieck's unpublished collection "Der lustige Erzähler guter Gesellschaft: Erstes Hundert lustiger Geschichten und Anekdoten."

641. Krassnig, Christl. "Tieck und die Musik: Ihre Stellung in Tiecks Werk." Diss. Vienna, 1944.

    Studies the manifestation and function of music in Tieck's works and sheds some light on his personal tastes regarding this art form. For a similar analysis, see no. 645.

642. Mittenzwei, Johannes. *Das Musikalische in der Literatur: Ein Überblick von Gottfried von Straßburg bis Brecht*. Halle (Saale): VEB Verlag Sprache und Literatur, 1962. 576 pp.

    Pp. 112-118 deal with Tieck's opinions on music, as expressed primarily in his contributions to *Phantasien über die Kunst*, as well as with "die Auflösung der Sprache in Musik" in a variety of his works.

643. Nahrebecky, Roman. *Wackenroder, Tieck, E.T.A. Hoffmann, Bettina von Arnim: Ihre Beziehung zur Musik und zum musikalischen Erlebnis*. Studien zur Germanistik, Anglistik und Komparatistik, Vol. 86. Bonn: Bouvier, 1979. 262 pp.

On pp. 37-86, comments on Tieck's relationship to music (which began with early violin lessons) and analyzes his three essays dealing with music in *Phantasien*, namely "Unmusikalische Toleranz," "Die Töne," and "Symphonien." Concludes that Tieck possessed less of an ear for music than Wackenroder, but that he did make the important point of arguing for music as a distinct art with its own merits.

644. Naumann, Barbara. *Musikalisches Ideen-Instrument: Das Musikalische in Poetik und Sprachtheorie der Frühromantik*. Stuttgart: J.B. Metzler, 1990. vii + 262 pp.

Contends that the poetological constructs of German Romanticism are based to a large extent on music and its associated terminology. In the case of Wackenroder and Tieck, Naumann's argumentation is founded primarily on *Phantasien über die Kunst*.

645. Schönewolf, Karl. "Ludwig Tieck und die Musik: Ein Beitrag zur Geschichte der deutschen Romantik." Diss. Marburg, 1923. Abstract in *Jahrbuch der philosophischen Fakultät der Philipps-Universität zu Marburg*, 1923/24, pp. 207-208.

A forerunnner of no. 641, this dissertation summarizes Tieck's views on music and discusses the concept of "innere Musik" as it applies to his works.

Cross ref.: 372, 632, 657.

## 3. EDUCATION

646. Apfelstedt, Hartmut. "Selbsterziehung und Selbstbildung in der deutschen Frühromantik: Friedrich Schlegel-Novalis-Wackenroder-Tieck." Diss. Munich, 1957.

Contains useful information on Tieck's utterances concerning education and especially self-actualization.

647. Kammradt, F. "Ludwig Tiecks Anschauungen über die Erziehung." *Zeitschrift für Geschichte der Erziehung und des Unterrichts*, 1 (1911): 233-273.

An overview of Tieck's rather unstructured philosophy on education.

## 4. PHILOSOPHY

648. Frank, Manfred. *Das Problem "Zeit" in der deutschen Romantik: Zeitbewußtsein und Bewußtsein von Zeitlichkeit in der frühromantischen Philosophie und in Tiecks Dichtung.* Munich: Winkler, 1972. 486 pp.

A carefully researched study on the romantic philosophy of time (as espoused by Friedrich Schlegel, Solger, and Novalis) and on its practical application in the works of Tieck.

649. Schmidt, W. "Fichtes Einfluß auf die ältere Romantik." *Euphorion*, 20 (1913): 435-458, 647-681; and 21 (1914): 251-270.

Pp. 253-255 of Vol. 21 (1914) are devoted to the influence of Fichte's philosophy on Tieck.

650. Schönebeck, Erich. *Tieck und Solger.* Berlin: Hermann Blanke, 1910. 87 pp.

On Tieck's indebtedness to the philosophy of K.W.F. Solger, particularly in his later novellas. For more on Solger's influence, see nos. 175 and 247.

## 5. POLITICS

651. Baxa, Jakob. "Ludwig Tieck und die Revolution. 1835." Pp. 166-168 in Baxa, *Einführung in die romantische Staatswissenschaft*. Jena: Gustav Fischer, 1923. 183 pp.

   Brief commentary concerning Tieck's views on the French Revolution and on politics and government in general.

652. Fink, Gonthier-Louis. "'Was ist ein Leben ohne Freiheit': Ludwig Tieck und die französische Revolution." Pp. 79-101 in *Les Romantiques allemands et la Révolution française: Actes du Colloque International*, ed. Gonthier-Louis Fink. Strassburg: Université des Sciences Humaines, 1989. 355 pp.

   The most comprehensive treatment available on the subject of Tieck and the French Revolution. Based extensively on source materials.

653. Jäger, Hans-Wolf. "Trägt Rotkäppchen eine Jakobiner-Mütze? Über mutmaßliche Konnotate bei Tieck und Grimm." Pp. 159-180 in *Literatursoziologie*, Vol. 2: *Beiträge zur Praxis*, ed. Joachim Bark. Stuttgart, Berlin, Cologne, Mainz: W. Kohlhammer, 1974. 195 pp.

   Probes the liberal and democratic sentiments expressed in the Riding Hood tales of Tieck and Grimm.

654. Oettinger, Klaus. "'Was ist ein Leben ohne Freiheit?': Jakobinertendenzen beim frühen Tieck." *Archiv für Kulturgeschichte*, 57 (1975): 412-425.

As a young man, Tieck supported the French Revolution and its underlying ideals.

Cross ref.: 210, 249, 383, 384.

## 6. RELIGION

655. Lang, Anthony Edgar. *Ludwig Tieck's Early Concept of Catholic Clergy and Church*. The Catholic University of America Studies in German, Vol. 8. Washington, D.C.: The Catholic University of America, 1936. xvi + 249 pp. Reprinted New York: AMS Press 1970.

    Tieck's "Catholicism" is evaluated both in literary and biographical terms, but without much critical insight.

656. Liepe, Wolfgang. *Das Religionsproblem im neueren Drama von Lessing bis zur Romantik*. Hermaea, Vol. 12. Halle a.d. Saale: Max Niemeyer, 1914. xviii + 267 pp. Reprinted Walluf bei Wiesbaden: Dr. Martin Sändig, 1972.

    Pp. 77-103, devoted to a study of the religious elements in *Genoveva* and *Octavianus*, also include a brief summary of Tieck's views on religion as expressed in earlier works.

657. Scheiber, Sister Mary Magdalita. *Ludwig Tieck and the Mediaeval Church*. The Catholic University of America Studies in German, Vol. 12. Washington, D.C.: The Catholic University of America Press, 1939. xix + 163 pp.

    Tieck glorified the medieval church in his works because it reminded him of "the good, old times of Germany." Of interest in this rather derivative study (compare with no. 655) is the commentary on Tieck and the "external features" of the church, which include art, architecture, and music.

Cross ref.: 458, 618, 619.

# XI. Reception, Influence, Comparative Studies

## 1. AMERICA

### a. General

658. Goodnight, Scott Holland. *German Literature in American Magazines Prior to 1846.* Madison: [University of Wisconsin], 1907. 264 pp.

   Lists 17 magazine articles and reviews dealing with Tieck and his works for the period before 1846. Continued in next item.

659. Haertel, Martin Henry. *German Literature in American Magazines 1846 to 1880.* Madison: [University of Wisconsin], 1908. 188 pp.

   This supplement to the previous item lists 12 magazine articles and reviews centering on Tieck and his oeuvre for the years 1846-1880.

660. Matenko, Percy. *Ludwig Tieck and America.* University of North Carolina Studies in Germanic Languages and

Literatures, Vol. 12. Chapel Hill: The University of North Carolina Press, 1954. xi + 120 pp.

Focuses on Tieck's American friends and visitors, on his reception in American books and magazines, and on American translations of his works. Wrongly assumes that books about America, as found on pp. 196-211 of the Asher catalogue (see no. 55), were part of Tieck's collection.

## b. Hawthorne

661. Alsen, Eberhard. "Poe's Theory of Hawthorne's Indebtedness to Tieck." *Anglia*, 91 (1973): 342-356.

    A highly speculative article attempting to disprove Poe's theory that Hawthorne's works were influenced by the fairy tales of Tieck (see also next item).

662. Baginski, Thomas. "Was Hawthorne a Puritan Tieck? Aspects of Nature Imagery in Hawthorne's *Tales* and Tieck's *Märchen*." *Literatur in Wissenschaft und Unterricht*, 18 (1985): 175-191.

    Supports the conclusions reached in the previous item via a discussion of the two authors' dissimilar usage of nature imagery.

663. Kern, Alfred A. "The Sources of Hawthorne's *Feathertop*." *PMLA*, 46 (1931): 1253-1259.

    Hints at the possibility that Tieck's novella "Die Vogelscheuche" (1835) may have influenced Hawthorne's "Feathertop" (1852).

664. Marks, Alfred H. "Hawthorne, Tieck, and Hoffmann: Adding to the Improbabilities of a Marvellous Tale." *ESQ: A Journal of the American Renaissance*, 35 (1989): 1-21.

At least as far as Tieck is concerned, this article represents a synthesis of the previous three items by contending that, while apparently no individual tale by Tieck or E.T.A. Hoffmann can be identified as an unmistakable source, Hawthorne was knowlegeable of the works of these men and copied their techniques vis-à-vis the application of particular literary styles, themes, and ornaments to transform "actualities into 'marvellous' tales."

## c. Loomis

665. Matenko, Percy. "Ludwig Tieck and Loomis' 'O'er the Sea.'" *Notes and Queries*, N.S. 3 (1956): 213.

   A note on a musical setting of Tieck's "Magelone" song "Geliebter, wo zaudert Dein irrender Fuss" by the American composer Harvey Worthington Loomis.

## d. Poe

666. Bohm, Arnd. "A German Source for Edgar Allan Poe's 'The Raven.'" *CLS*, 23 (1986): 310-323.

   Argues convincingly that Tieck's poem "Phantasus" (1812) had a direct influence on Poe's "Raven" (1845).

667. Lewis, Paul. "The Intellectual Functions of Gothic Fiction: Poe's 'Ligeia' and Tieck's 'Wake Not the Dead.'" *CLS*, 16 (1979): 207-221.

   A somewhat inconclusive study of Poe's indebtedness to Tieck.

668. Zeydel, Edwin H. "Edgar Allen Poe's Contacts with German as Seen in his Relations with Ludwig Tieck." Pp. 47-54 in *Studies in German Literature of the Nineteenth and Twentieth Centuries: Festschrift for Frederic E. Coenen*, ed. Siegfried Mews. University of North Car-

olina Studies in the Germanic Languages and Literatures, Vol. 67. Chapel Hill: The University of North Carolina Press, 1970. xx + 251 pp.

In contrast to the previous two items, asserts that any influence of Tieck upon Poe could only have occurred via secondary British and American sources, since Poe is not known to have read Tieck in the original.

## 2. BRITAIN

### a. General

669. Boening, John, ed. *The Reception of Classical German Literature in England, 1760-1860: A Documentary History from Contemporary Periodicals*, Vols. 1, 2, 3, 5, and 6. New York, London: Garland, 1977. xxxiv + 567, xv + 457, xv + 565, xix + 677, xiii + 539 pp.

Good facsimilie collection of English reviews of German literature. Vols. 1, 2, 3, and 5 contain briefer mentions of Tieck within the greater context of contemporary German literature, while vol. 6 (items 67-90) contains the more important reviews devoted to individual works by Tieck. The latter reviews range in date from 1801-1856.

670. Zeydel, Edwin H. *Ludwig Tieck and England: A Study in the Literary Relations of Germany and England During the Early Nineteenth Century*. Princeton: Princeton University Press, 1931. vii + 264 pp.

This useful reception study holds information on Tieck's travels to England, his English visitors and correspondents, and his collection of English books. Based in part on unpublished source materials.

## b. Coleridge

671. Bidney, Martin. "Beneficent Birds and Crossbow Crimes: The Nightmare-Confessions of Coleridge and Ludwig Tieck." *Papers on Language & Literature*, 25 (1989): 44-58.

   A comparison between Tieck's "Eckbert" and Coleridge's "The Rime of the Ancient Mariner," both from 1797. Shows that, while there can be no assumption of any sort of influence, both works treat guilt, loneliness, and self-persecution in much the same way, even sharing several visual images.

672. Stokoe, F.W. *German Influence in the English Romantic Period 1788-1818: With Special Reference to Scott, Coleridge, Shelley and Byron*. Cambridge: Cambridge University Press, 1926. x + 202 pp.

   Pp. 123-127 contain a unique comparison between the prose version of Coleridge's "Glycine's Song" and Tieck's "Herbstlied." Stokoe concludes that Coleridge's poem, dating from the early nineteenth century, was definitely influenced by that of Tieck, which was written between 1793 and 1799.

## c. Shakespeare

673. Pfeiffer, Emilie. *Shakespeares und Tiecks Märchendramen*, Mnemosyne, Vol. 13. Bonn: n.p., 1933. 84 pp.

   A comparative study pointing to the existence of both baroque and romantic elements in the dramas of Shakespeare and Tieck.

## d. Webster

674. Koskenniemi, Inna. *John Webster's "The White Devil" and Ludwig Tieck's "Vittoria Accorombona": A*

*Study of two Related Works.* Turun Yliopiston Julkaisuja, Series B, Vol. 97. Turku: Turun Yliopisto, 1966. 51 pp.

Shared themes and historical sources make up the bulk of this comparative analysis.

### e. Wilde

675. Corkhill, Alan. "Tiecks *William Lovell* und Wildes *The Picture of Dorian Gray*: Eine kontinuierliche Tradition." *Archiv*, 224 (1987): 346-352.

Shows that Wilde's narcissistic, bored protagonist is closely related to – and may have been influenced by – Tieck's "Lovell-Typ."

## 3. FRANCE

### a. General

676. Lambert, José. *Ludwig Tieck dans les lettres françaises: Aspects d'une résistance au romantisme allemand.* Etudes de litterature etrangere et comparee. Louvain: Presses Universitaires de Louvain, Librairie Marcel Didier, 1976. ix + 488 pp.

Expanding on no. 678, thoroughly documents Tieck's declining fortunes in France during the nineteenth century. Includes an extensive bibliography, particularly in terms of French Tieck translations.

677. Maurer, Maria. "Ludwig Tieck und Frankreich." Diss. Vienna, 1943.

While this superficial study addresses itself to Tieck's attitude towards France and to his indebtedness to French literature, it focuses primarily on his reception by French critics.

678. Teichmann, Elisabeth. "Tieck in Frankreich oder 'Die Fahrt ins Blaue hinein': 1800-1850." *RLC*, 37 (1963): 513-539.

Despite Tieck's popularity among such critics as Ampère and Marmier, his works did not enjoy a wide readership in nineteenth century France, due in part to poor translations (see also no. 676).

**b. Flaubert**

679. Stanley, Robert. "Tieck's *Der blonde Eckbert* and Flaubert's *Saint Julien*: Blood and Guilt in Two Tales." *Journal of Evolutionary Psychology*, 5 (1984): 245-254.

Compares Tieck's "Eckbert" (1797) to Flaubert's *Saint Julien* (1877) and finds many similarities in terms of style, setting, protagonists, psychological implications, and content. Does not infer from this, however, that Flaubert was in any way influenced by Tieck.

**c. Zola**

680. Whiting, George W. "*Volpone, Herr von Fuchs*, and *Les Héritiers Rabourdin*." *PMLA*, 46 (1931): 605-607.

Works by Jonson and Tieck are suggested as sources for Zola's *Les Héritiers Rabourdin*.

## 4. GERMANY

**a. General**

681. Altenhein, Richard. *Ludwig Tieck als Berater der Jugend: Ein Beitrag zur ausgehenden Romantik*. Bonn: Paul Rost, 1921. 15 pp. Excerpt of Diss. Bonn, 1921.

Tieck's influence on a number of authors from the late romantic and early realistic periods, including Alexis, Freytag, Grabbe, Hebbel, Immermann, Laube, Menzel, Mosen, and Uechtritz.

682. Fischer, Hermann. "Ludwig Tieck und seine schwäbischen Jünger." *Deutsche Rundschau*, 165 (1915): 217-232.

An influence study focusing primarily on the Swabian romantics. Heavily biased against Tieck.

683. Hewett-Thayer, Harvey W. "Tieck's Novellen and Contemporary Journalistic Criticism." *GR*, 3 (1928): 328-360.

Provides a general survey of the critical reception of Tieck's later novellas in representative German newspapers and magazines from the period 1820-1840. Shows that, as time went by, the novellas became increasingly unpopular because of their often reactionary content.

684. Klett, Dwight A. *Tieck-Rezeption: Das Bild Ludwig Tiecks in den deutschen Literaturgeschichten des 19. Jahrhunderts*. Beiträge zur neueren Literaturgeschichte, N.S. 3, Vol. 79. Heidelberg: Carl Winter, 1989. 127 pp.

A detailed reception study accompanied by a comprehensive bibliography of nineteenth century German literary histories containing information on Tieck.

685. Mazur, Gertrud S. "Ein Stiefkind der deutschen Literaturkritik: Ludwig Tieck." *Selecta*, 2 (1981): 55-58.

   Points out injustices in the German criticism surrounding Tieck.

686. Paulin, Roger. "Die Textillustrationen der Riepenhausens zu Tiecks 'Genoveva': Wirkungen der bildenden Kunst auf die Rezeption eines Werkes romantischer Literatur." *Aurora*, 38 (1978): 32-53.

   The *Genoveva* illustrations by the Riepenhausens not only influenced the reception of this particular work, but also of Tieck's entire oeuvre.

687. Peschken, Bernd. *Versuch einer germanistischen Ideologiekritik: Goethe, Lessing, Novalis, Tieck, Hölderlin, Heine in Wilhelm Diltheys und Julian Schmidts Vorstellungen*. Texte Metzler, Vol. 23. Stuttgart: J.B. Metzler, 1972. 195 pp.

   Contains information on the portrayal of Tieck in historical writings by Dilthey and Schmidt (see also no. 684).

688. Schmidt, Arno. *"Funfzehn": Vom Wunderkind der Sinnlosigkeit*. Pp. 208-281 in Schmidt, *Die Ritter vom Geist: Von vergessenen Kollegen*. Karlsruhe: Stahlberg, 1965. 316 pp. Reprinted Frankfurt am Main: S. Fischer, 1985.

   A satiric drama centering on Tieck's life and its frequent misinterpretation by German critics. Argues that Tieck was never truly recognized as a national author in Germany and that much more has been contributed to the rehabilitation of his image by foreign scholars than by their German counterparts.

689. Werner, Karl. "Ein Roman vor 100 Jahren." *Beilage zur Allgemeinen Zeitung*, Munich, 17 August 1898, pp. 1-4.

Vividly demonstrates how public opinion regarding *Franz Sternbalds Wanderungen* changed in the 100 years following its initial publication in 1798.

Cross ref.: 57, 196, 200, 211, 291, 375, 420, 563.

**b. Goethe**

690. Francke, Kuno. "A Parallel to Goethe's Euphorion." *MLN*, 10 (1895): 65-66.

    On similarities between Tieck's poem "Phantasus" (1812) and numerous verses in part two of Goethe's *Faust*.

691. Porterfield, Allen W. "Goethe and Tieck: A Study in Dramatic Parallels." *JEGP*, 36 (1937): 66-82.

    A strained comparison between Goethe's *Der Triumph der Empfindsamkeit* (1787) and Tieck's *Prinz Zerbino* (1799).

Cross ref.: 110.

**c. Schiller**

692. Borchert, Hans Heinrich, ed. *Schiller und die Romantiker: Briefe und Dokumente*. Stuttgart: J.G. Cotta, 1948. 760 pp.

    On pp. 80-92 and 604-626, demonstrates via source materials that Schiller did not hold Tieck's works in high esteem, believing them to be products of a wasted talent.

693. Minor, Jacob. "Zu Schillers 'Spaziergang' und Tiecks 'gestiefeltem Kater.'" *ZDP*, 20 (1888): 75.

    A note concluding that the similarities between these two works in no way prove any sort of mutual influence.

694. Sulger-Gebing, Emil. "Schillers Entwurf 'Rosamund oder die Braut der Hölle.'" *Euphorion*, 19 (1912): 148-174.

Identifies Tieck's "Briefe über W. Shakespeare" (1800) as a major source for a ballad by Schiller (also 1800), which is discussed here in its manuscript form.

### d. Wieland

695. Melz, Fritz. "Wieland und Tieck: Ein Verleich." Diss. University of California, 1936.

A general comparative study focusing on themes, styles, and both enlightened and romantic elements in works by the two authors. Due for an update.

696. Tecchi, Bonaventura. "La fiaba nell'opera di Wieland e in quella di Tieck." *Studi Germanici*, N.S. 3 (1965): 301-320.

Compares Tieck's "Kunstmärchen" to the tales of Wieland.

### e. Romantic Generation

#### i. Brentano

697. Böckmann, Paul. "Die romantische Poesie Brentanos und ihre Grundlagen bei Friedrich Schlegel und Tieck: Ein Beitrag zur Entwicklung der Formensprache der deutschen Romantik." *JFDH*, 1934/35, pp. 56-176.

An important influence study that acknowledges Tieck's leadership position within German Romanticism, particularly where "die dichterische Praxis" is concerned.

698. Nippold, Erich. *Tiecks Einfluss auf Brentano*. Weida in Thür.: Thomas & Hubert, 1915. 81 pp.

Brentano was most heavily inspired by Tieck – especially in terms of literary themes – during the years 1799-1805, when he wrote such works as *Godwi* and *Ponce de Leon*.

### ii. Eichendorff

699. Fiedler, Herta. "Das Verhältnis Eichendorffs zu Tieck in seinen erzählenden Dichtungen." Diss. Prague, 1929.

The only, albeit outdated and virtually inaccessible, book-length study comparing Eichendorff's prose works to those of Tieck. Needs revision.

700. Lindemann, Klaus. "Von der Naturphilosophie zur christlichen Kunst: Zur Funktion des Venusmotivs in Tiecks 'Runenberg' und Eichendorffs 'Marmorbild.'" *LJGG*, N.S. 15 (1974): 101-124.

A useful comparative study centering on the portrayal of Venus in the two named tales. Does not rule out the possibility that Eichendorff may have been influenced by Tieck.

701. Purver, Judith. "Wild Women: A Comparison of Interpolated Narratives in Tieck's *Das Zauberschloß* and Eichendorff's *Dichter und ihre Gesellen*." *GL&L*, N.S. 40 (1987): 117-134.

Compares Tieck's "Die wilde Engländerin," a story within his novella "Das Zauberschloß" (1830), with Eichendorff's "Geschichte der wilden Spanierin," which appears as part of his novel *Dichter und ihre Gesellen* (1834). Purver indicates that, while Eichendorff certainly used Tieck's story as a source, he totally reshaped it "in accordance with the requirements of his own fictional world."

*iii*. Novalis

702. Kahn, Robert L. "Tieck's *Franz Sternbalds Wanderungen* and Novalis' *Heinrich von Ofterdingen*." *SIR*, 7 (1967/68): 40-64.

An evaluation of the two "Bildungsromane" yielding the conclusion that, although Novalis' work was influenced considerably by that of Tieck, it far surpassed its model both in thematic and stylistic terms.

703. Lagutina, I.N. "Obraz khudozhnika v romanakh Liudviga Tika 'Stranstvovaniia Frantsa Shternbal'da' i Novalisa 'Genrikh fon Ofterdingen.'" *VMU*, No. 3 (1990): 58-63.

Like the preceding item, a comparison between the two novels, this time with emphasis on the role and presentation of artists.

*iv*. Others
(Arnim, E.T.A. Hoffmann, Schumann)

704. Billington, Steven Miles. "Robert Schumann's 'Genoveva': A Source Study." Diss. New York University, 1987. Abstract in *DAI*, 481, No. 11A (1988): 2756.

Tieck's *Genoveva* is considered as one of the important sources for Schumann's opera.

705. Jost, Walter. *Von Ludwig Tieck zu E.T.A. Hoffmann: Studien zur Entwicklungsgeschichte des romantischen Subjektivismus*. Deutsche Forschungen, Vol. 4. Frankfurt am Main: Moritz Diesterweg, 1921. x + 139 pp. Reprinted Darmstadt: Wissenschaftliche Buchgesellschaft, 1969.

Hoffmann was greatly influenced by the works of both Tieck and Wackenroder, particularly when it comes to music, irony, romantic longing, and fairy tale forms.

706. Schirmunski, Victor. "Kümmermann – Ludwig Tieck." *GRM*, 10 (1922): 375-377.

Attempts to prove that the cantankerous character Kümmermann in Achim von Arnim's drama *Halle und Jerusalem* (1811) is modelled after Tieck.

Cross ref.: 620-624 (Runge), 682 (Swabian romantics).

**f. Young Germany**

*i*. Heine

707. Elstner, Ernst. "Das Vorbild der freien Rythmen Heinrich Heines." *Euphorion*, 25 (1924): 63-86.

On the influence of Tieck's *Reisegedichte* on Heine's free verse.

708. Linde, Otto zur. *Heine und die deutsche Romantik*. Freiburg: C.A. Wagner, 1899. iii + 219 pp.

Includes notes on Heine's reception of Tieck and points out similarities between the works of the two men.

*ii*. Others
(Gutzkow, Laube)

709. Kurz, Marlies. "Ludwig Tiecks und Heinrich Laubes Stellung zur Schauspielkunst: Eine vergleichende Gegenüberstellung." Diss. Munich, 1951.

A comparison between the dramaturgical principles of Tieck and Laube, which – from a biographical standpoint – treats Tieck unfairly (see also no. 681).

710. Wohlrab, Anna. "Karl Gutzkow als Novellist in seinem Verhältnis zu Ludwig Tieck." Diss. Vienna, 1948.

Praises Tieck as a "Meister der Novelle" and shows how and where he influenced Gutzkow.

## g. Realists

### *i.* Hebbel

711. Hewett-Thayer, Harvey W. "Ludwig Tieck and Hebbel's Tragedy of Beauty." *GR*, 2 (1927): 16-25.

Speculates that Tieck's *Accorombona* (1840) may have been a source for Hebbel's *Agnes Bernauer* (1855).

712. Klenze, Camillo von. "Zu Tieck und Hebbel." *Euphorion*, 20 (1913): 165-166.

General note on similarities between the two men's works.

Cross ref.: 681.

### *ii.* Immermann

713. Küper, Walther. *Immermanns Verhältnis zur Frühromantik unter besonderer Berücksichtigung seiner Beziehungen zu Ludwig Tieck*. Münster: Regensbergsche Buchdruckerei, 1913. 67 pp.

Immermann's reorganization of the Düsseldorf theater was inspired to a large extent by Tieck.

714. Wohnlich, Oskar. *Tiecks Einfluß auf Immermann besonders auf seine epische Produktion*. Sprache und Dichtung, Vol. 11. Tübingen: J.C.B. Mohr (Paul Siebeck), 1913. xi + 72 pp.

Discusses parallels between the later fiction of Tieck and that of Immermann.

Cross ref.: 681.

### iii. Others
### (Grabbe, Ludwig, Mörike, Raabe)

715. Berend, Eduard. "Mörike auf Tiecks Spuren." *JDSG*, 12 (1968): 315-317.

   A note on "romantische Illusionsstörungen" via a comparison between Mörike's humorous poem "Häusliche Szene" (1853) and a scene from Tieck's comedy *Prinz Zerbino* (1799).

716. Greiner, Wilhelm. *Die ersten Novellen Otto Ludwigs und ihr Verhältnis zu Ludwig Tieck*. Pössneck i. Th.: Bruno Feigenspan, 1903. 51 pp.

   Echoes of Tieck can be found in the early novellas of Ludwig.

717. Huth, Otto. *Raabe und Tieck*. Wilhelm Raabe-Studien, Vol. 1. Essen: Die blaue Eule, 1985. 76 pp.

   Focuses on the influence of Tieck's novella "Der funfzehnte November" (1827) and, above all, its "Sintflutsymbolik," on Raabe's *Die Chronik der Sperlingsgasse* (1857) and *Stopfkuchen* (1891).

718. Moes, Eberhard. *Christian Dietrich Grabbes Dramen im Wandel der Urteile von Ludwig Tieck bis zur Gegenwart*. Borna-Leipzig: Robert Noske, 1929. 52 pp.

   Includes a few superficial comments concerning Tieck's influence on and perception of Grabbe's dramas (see also no. 681).

**h. Others**

> *i.* Eighteenth and Nineteenth Century
> (Carus, Jean Paul, Maler Müller)

719. Klett, Dwight A. "Carl Gustav Carus' Physiognomic Assessment of Tieck and its Value for Modern Scholarship (With a Discussion of Carus' Influence on Tieck's Novella 'Der funfzehnte November')." *Selected Proceedings of the Pennsylvania Foreign Language Conference*, 3 (1991/92): [p. nos. unavailable at time of printing].

On Carus' reception of Tieck via a letter found in no. 15. Contains a physiognomic interpretation of "Der funfzehnte November," a work most probably influenced by Carus.

720. Schneider, F.J. "Tiecks 'William Lovell' und Jean Pauls 'Titan.'" *ZDP*, 61 (1936): 58-75.

This comparative study yields the conclusion that *Titan* (1800-1803) was heavily indebted to *Lovell* (1795-1796) in the areas of content, themes, and style.

721. Seyboth, Hermann. *Dramatische Technik und Weltanschauung in Tiecks "Genoveva" und Maler Müllers "Golo und Genoveva."* Regensburg: Heinrich Schiele, 1928. 65 pp.

A comparison showing that Tieck's play is more spiritual in nature than that of Müller.

> *ii.* Twentieth Century
> (Kafka)

722. Corkhill, Alan. "Tiecks *Blonder Eckbert* und Kafkas *Urteil*: Textliche Übereinstimmungen." *Literatur in Wissenschaft und Unterricht*, 18 (1985): 1-11.

Points to thematic and ideological parallels in the named works by Tieck and Kafka, but not necessarily to any sort of influence on Tieck's part.

## 5. ITALY

723. Fasola, Carlo. "Ludwig Tieck in Italia." *Revista mensile di letteratura tedesca*, 1 (1907): 159-161.

    Briefly introduces a number of Italian translations of Tieck's works.

724. Poggi, Tamara Baikova. "Ludwig Tieck, un anello di congiunzione tra Nikolaj Evreinov e Luigi Pirandello." Pp. 132-148 in *Elemente der Literatur: Beiträge zur Stoff-, Motiv- und Themenforschung. Elisabeth Frenzel zum 65. Geburtstag*, ed. Adam J. Bisanz and Raymond Trousson, Vol. 2. Kröner Themata, Vol. 703. Stuttgart: Kröner, 1980. 177 pp.

    Concerning Tieck's influence on the modern Italian and, to a lesser extent, Russian theater.

## 6. RUSSIA

725. Stender-Petersen, A. "Gogol und die deutsche Romantik." *Euphorion*, 24 (1922): 628-653.

    Works by E.T.A. Hoffmann and especially Tieck are identified as sources for the novellas of the early Russian realist. One of only a few useful contributions to the history of German-Russian literary relations.

Cross ref.: 724.

## 7. SWEDEN

726. Santesson, Carl. "Tiecks prosa och 'Lycksalighetens ö.'" *Samlaren: Tidskrift för svensk litteraturhistorisk forskning*, N.S. 7 (1926): 109-127.

   An insightful article concerning Tieck's impact on the works of Per Atterbom, the father of Swedish Romanticism (see also next item).

727. Vetterlund, Fredrik. "En sagodikt av Tieck – och 'Lycksalighetens ö': En opåaktad parallell." *Samlaren: Tidskrift för svensk litteraturhistorisk forskning*, N.S. 21 (1940): 119-124.

   A comparative study building on the previous item.

# Index of Authors and Editors

Alewyn, Richard 82, 626
Alsen, Eberhard 661
Altenhein, Richard 681
Alverdes, Paul 211
Amon, Clara 258
Apfelstedt, Hartmut 646
Arendt, Dieter 234
Arnold, Paul Joh. 235
Arntzen, Helmut 194, 267
Asper, Helmut G. 566
Assing, Ludmilla 535
Atkinson, Margaret E. 639
Aubert, Andreas 620

Baginski, Thomas 662
Baldensperger, Fernand 536
Bamberg, Felix 537
Bastier, Paul 558
Bauer, Frieda 342
Baumgärtner, Alfred Clemens 387
Baus, Lothar 9
Baxa, Jakob 651
Becker, Marta 507
Beckers, Gustav 403

Beckmann, Heinz 200
Begemann, Christian 324
Behler, Ernst 219
Behrmann, Alfred 213
Belgardt, Raimund 388
Bent, M.I. 399
Berend, Eduard 715
Bergmann, Alfred 538, 539
Bernays, Michael 600
Bernhardi, Wilhelm 10
Bertrand, J.-J.A. 113, 220, 327, 380
Beutel, Georg 34
Beyer, Hans Georg 201
Bidney, Martin 671
Biesterfeld, Wolfgang 202
Billington, Steven Miles 704
Binder, Franz 491
Birrell, Gordon 268
Bischoff, Heinrich 559
Blackall, Eric A. 400
Blaze [de Bury], Henri 35
Bloesch, Hans 343
Bock, Alfred 66
Bodensohn, Anneliese 230

Böckmann, Paul 152, 697
Böhme, Hartmut 269
Boening, John 669
Bohm, Arnd 666
Bolte, Johannes 640
Borchert, Hans Heinrich 692
Bosch, Eva 616
Brandt, Heinrich 579
Branky, Franz 612
Brinker-Gabler, Gisela 25, 517, 585, 586
Brion, Marcel 90
Brodnitz, Käthe 184
Brömel, Karl 430
Brüggemann, Fritz 404
Brüggemann, Joseph 611
Brüggemann, Werner 221, 396
Brummack, Jürgen 132
Brunner, Horst 181
Budde, Josef 138
Bürger, Christa 292, 293
Busch, Willi 127

Campe, Elisabeth 540
Carus, C.G. 36
Churbanova, V.S. 236
Cohn, Alfons Fedor 26, 541
Coleridge, Ernest Hartley 529
Conen, Franz 348
Corkhill, Alan 128, 182, 405, 675, 722
Crisman, William 270, 271
Croce, Elena Craveri 91
Cullmann, Rudolf 617

Danton, George Henry 140, 431, 633
Davies, J.M.Q. 294

Delius, N. 567
Diez, Max 328
Dingelstedt, Franz 512
Donat, Walter 141
Donner, J.O.E. 237
Drach, Erich 560
Dux, Karl 225

Ederheimer, Edgar 107
Eichler, Albert 373
Ellis, John M. 295
Elstner, Ernst 707
Endrulat, Helmut 349
Erny, Richard 153
Esselborn, Hans 406
Etscheidt, Lotte 502
Eulenberg, Herbert 37, 38
Ewald, Karl 350
Ewers, Hans-Heino 401
Ewton, Ralph W., Jr. 296, 329

Faerber, Ludwig 133
Falkenberg, Hans-Geert 1
Fambach, Oscar 488
Fasola, Carlo 723
Favier, Georges 341
Fehling, Maria 520
Feilchenfeldt, Konrad 621
Fickert, Kurt J. 297
Fiebiger, Otto 503, 542
Fiedler, Herta 699
Field, Jean Clark 129
Fife, Robert Herndon 473
Fink, Gonthier-Louis 259, 272, 330, 432, 652
Finke, Heinrich 482
Finney, Gail 298
Fischer, Elfriede 351
Fischer, Hermann 682

Fischer, Jens Malte 238
Fischer, L.H 48
Fischer, Ottokar 121
Fischer, Walther 568
Fischer, Wolfram 32
Fiumi, Annamaria Borsano 569
Flatter, Richard 601
Förster, Ernst 479
Fränkel, Ludwig 27
Francke, Kuno 407, 690
Frank, Manfred 11, 648
Franke, Christa 622
Freiberg, Günther von 39
Frerking, Johann 214
Freund, Winfried 299
Freye, Karl 594
Friedrich, Werner P. 212
Fries, Thomas 300
Friesen, Hermann Freiherr von 40
Fritz-Grandjean, Sonia 144
Fritze, Franz 543
Frommann, Friedrich Johannes 521
Frye, Lawrence O. 331

Galaski, Lisa 215
Garmann, Garburg 239
Garnier, T.D. 240
Geiger, Ludwig 498
Gellinek, Janis Little 301
Gentges, Ignaz 195
Genton, Elisabeth 528
Geulen, Hans 433
Geyder, August 522
Gillespie, Gerald 196, 241
Gillies, A. 28, 29
Gish, Theodore 260
Gladow, Gudrun 627

Gliwitzky, Hans 513
Gneuss, Christian 352
Gnüg, Hiltrud 154
Görte, Erna 108
Goldfriedrich, J. 523
Goodnight, Scott Holland 658
Gorm, Ludwig 226
Gottrau, André 242
Gould, Robert 389
Graef, Hermann 12
Greiner, Bernhard 302
Greiner, Martin 155
Greiner, Wilhelm 716
Gries, Frauke 553, 581, 582
Griggs, Earl Leslie 530
Gross, Edgar 561
Grünbaum, Anita 570
Grundy, J.B.C. 623
Grunewald, Eckhard 634
Günther, Hans 134, 524
Günther, Johannes 562
Günzel, Klaus 13
Gumbel, Hermann 83
Gundolf, Friedrich 92
Guretzky-Cornitz, Ulrike von 408

Haase, Donald P. 273
Haenicke, Diether H. 303
Haertel, Martin Henry 659
Härtl, Heinz 172
Haeuptner, Gerhard 304
Hahn, R.E. 41
Hahn, Walther L. 305, 390
Halter, Ernst 231
Hammes, Michael Paul 119
Hardy, Swana L. 222
Harnisch, Käthe 434
Hartmann, Hans 618

Hartmann, Julius 492
Hasinski, Maksymilian 344
Hasselbach, Karlheinz 306
Hassler, Karl 409
Hauffen, Adolf 56
Haußmann, J.F. 122
Haym, Rudolf 93
Hecker, Max 374
Heinichen, Jürgen 353
Heinisch, Klaus J. 307, 382
Hellge, Rosemarie 150
Hemmer, Heinrich 130
Hense, C.C. 216
Hering, Christoph 429
Hertel, Theodor 325
Herzog, Wilhelm 410
Hettner, Hermann 554
Hewett-Thayer, Harvey W. 197, 555, 571, 683, 711
Hibberd, J.L. 435
Hienger, Jörg 354
Hille, Curt 185
Hille, Gertrud 572
Hillmann, Heinz 94
Hock, Stefan 183
Hoeft, Bernhard 14
Hölter, Achim 30, 57
Hoermann, Roland 436
Hoffmann, J.L. 84
Hoffmann von Fallersleben, August Heinrich 544
Hoffner, Wilhelm 77
Holtei, Karl von 467, 468
Horton, David 308
Horton, Gudrun 145
Houben, Heinrich Hubert 511, 545
Hubbs, V.C. 274, 309
Hubert, Ulrich 397
Hummer, Margarethe 355

Huth, Otto 717

Immerwahr, Raymond M. 189, 203, 310, 311

Jacobs, Jürgen 243, 615
Jäger, Hans-Wolf 653
Joachimi-Dege, Marie 573
Jost, François 411, 412
Jost, Walter 602, 705

Kahn, Ludwig W. 603
Kahn, Robert L. 702
Kaiser, Oscar 173
Kammradt, F. 647
Kamphausen, A. 437
Kanzog, Klaus 78, 79, 595
Kasack, Hermann 95
Katz, Moritz 123
Kauf, Robert 312
Kausler, Rudolph 96
Keck, Christiane E. 453
Kemme, Hans-Martin 563
Kempf, Thomas 438
Kerber, Erich 574
Kern, Alfred A. 663
Kern, Hanspeter 223, 224
Kern, Johannes P. 85
Kerner, Theobald 493
Kiel, Hanna 345
Kienzerle, Renate 156
Kiesant, Knut 590
Kimmerich, Peter 356
Kimpel, Dieter 413
Kimpel, Richard W. 275
Klee, Gotthold 169, 474, 475, 587
Klein, Johannes 357
Klenze, Camillo von 712
Klett, Dwight A. 376, 684,

719
Kluckhohn, Paul 174
Kluge, Gerhard 157
Klussmann, Paul Gerhard 86, 160, 244, 276, 358
Knight, Victor 332
Knopper, Françoise 414, 415
Knudsen, Hans 346
Koch, Max 575
Köhler, Reinhold 596
König, Bernhard 613
Köpke, Rudolf 15
Körner, Josef 161, 483, 499, 533, 588
Kohlschmidt, Werner 628, 629
Koldewey, Paul 109
Koopmann, Helmut 384
Koskenniemi, Inna 674
Kraft, Herbert 177
Krassnig, Christl 641
Krauß, Rudolf 67
Krebs, Siegfried 624
Kremer, Detlef 333
Kreuzer, Helmut 204
Kreuzer, Ingrid 245
Kröll, Joachim 31
Krohn, Rüdiger 591
Kronacher, Bettina 614
Küper, Walther 713
Kummer, Friedrich 580
Kurrelmeyer, W. 500
Kurz, Marlies 709

Lagutina, I.N. 703
Lambert, José 75, 676
Landau, Marcus 454
Lang, Anthony Edgar 655
Langermann, H. von 604
Larson, Kenneth E. 605

Laube, Heinrich 347
Laun, Friedrich 504
Lauth, Reinhard 513
Lebede, Hans 449
Leppmann, Franz 205
Lewis, Paul 667
Lewy, Käthe 359
Leyen, Friedrich von der 489
Liedke, Otto K. 313
Liepe, Wolfgang 656
Lieske, Rudolf 97
Lillyman, William J. 246, 314, 334, 391, 439, 455
Linde, Otto zur 708
Lindemann, Klaus 700
Lindig, Horst 402
Linn, Rolf N. 392
Lippuner, Heinz 630
Littlejohns, Richard 261, 463, 490, 609, 635
Lohner, Edgar 484
Loquai, Franz 162
Ludwig, Albert 375
Lüdeke, H. 485, 515, 576, 606
Lüdtke, Ernst 232
Lussky, Alfred Edwin 98, 114, 139

Maassen, C.G. von 262, 610
Maelsaecke, Dirk van 416
Mai, Andrea Angela 116
Maione, Italo 16
Manacorda, Guido 163
Marelli, Adriana 186
Marks, Alfred H. 664
Marquardt, Hertha 59
Masche, Bertha 470
Mason, Eudo C. 60
Matenko, Percy 68, 76, 170, 379, 466, 469, 470, 473,

510, 514, 516, 526, 534, 660, 665
Matinian, K.R. 206
Maurer, Maria 677
Mazur, Gertrud S. 277, 685
McKinstry, Brian Edmund John 383
Mecklenburg, Norbert 335
Meisner, Heinrich 546, 547
Melz, Fritz 695
Meuthen, Erich 440
Meves, Uwe 589
Miessner, Wilhelm 158
Minder, Robert 3-5, 17, 18
Minor, Jacob 110, 360, 693
Mittenzwei, Johannes 642
Mittner, Ladislao 164
Mörtl, Hans 247, 385, 456
Moes, Eberhard 718
Mornin, Edward 441, 442
Mühl, Beate 248
Müller, Gustav Adolf 525
Müller, Joachim 377
Müller-Dyes, Klaus 278, 279
Münz, Walter 417

Nabbe, Hildegard 625, 636, 637
Nahrebecky, Roman 643
Naumann, Barbara 644
Naumann, Walter 165
Nef, Ernst 190
Nehrkorn, Hans 398
Neuburger, Paul 159
Neunzig, Hans A. 19
Nippold, Erich 698
Nobuoka, Yorio 280, 371
Nollendorfs, Cora Lee 326
Northcott, Kenneth J. 315

Oesterle, Ingrid 393
Oettinger, Klaus 654
Ottmann, Dagmar 361

Paulin, Roger 2, 6, 20, 42, 99, 249, 556, 592, 638, 686
Paulsell, Patricia R. 207
Peschken, Bernd 687
Pestalozzi, Karl 208
Petersen, Julius 577
Petrich, Hermann 117
Peuker, Klaus 281
Pfeiffer, Emilie 673
Pietsch, Ludwig 49
Pikulik, Lothar 146, 418
Poggi, Tamara Baikova 724
Pongs, Hermann 282
Porterfield, Allen W. 450, 691
Pratas, Maria 381
Prodnigg, Heinrich 443
Prölss, Robert 578
Proskauer, Paul F. 419
Purver, Judith 701

Ranftl, Johann 227
Rank, Otto 136
Rasch, Wolfdietrich 336
Raumer, Friedrich von 508, 509
Regener, Edgar Alfred 179
Rehm, Walther 457
Reichel, Otto 518
Reinhard, Ewald 69, 209
Reitmeyer, Elisabeth 166
Rek, Klaus 21
Rellstab, L. 50
Retland, J. Florus 551, 552
Ribbat, Ernst 87, 111, 135, 444

Richer, Jean 340
Richter, Fritz K. 451
Riederer, Frank 593
Riha, Karl 420
Rippere, Victoria L. 316
Roetteken, Hubert 445
Rosenkranz, Karl 100
Rowley, Brian A. 124, 250
Rózycki, K. von 43
Rübsam, Gertraut Mathilde 228
Rüter, Hubert 583
Runge, Johann Daniel 494
Rusack, Hedwig Hoffmann 187
Rutz, Wilhelm 394

Sammons, Jeffrey L. 446
Samuel, Richard 526
Sanders, Daniel 369, 370
Santesson, Carl 726
Santoli, Vittorio 631
Sapozhkov, S.V. 233
Sartori, Gemma 167
Schack, Adolf Friedrich Graf von 22
Scharnowski, Susanne 421
Schaum, Marta 362
Scheck, Ulrich 422
Scheibe, Friedrich Carl 251
Scheiber, Sister Mary Magdalita 657
Schemann, Ludwig 548
Scherer, G. 44
Scherer, Michael 252
Scheuer, Helmut 265
Schirmunski, Victor 706
Schläfer, Ute 363
Schlaffer, Heinz 317
Schmidt, Arno 688

Schmidt, Erich 378, 546, 547
Schmidt, Thomas E. 447
Schmidt, W. 649
Schneider, Albert 229
Schneider, F.J. 720
Schönebeck, Erich 650
Schönewolf, Karl 645
Scholte, J.H. 584
Schoolfield, George C. 372
Schröder, Rolf 364
Schüddekopf, Carl 478
Schürk, Brigitte 253
Schütz, Wilhelm von 458
Schulz, Eberhard Wilhelm 448
Schulz, W. 607
Schumacher, Hans 283
Schunicht, Manfred 254
Schwarzlose, Walter 564
Schweikert, Uwe 80, 151, 471, 472, 480
Schwering, Markus 386
Segebrecht, Wulf 88, 160, 495, 505
Sellner, Timothy F. 318
Sergel, Albert 74
Seyboth, Hermann 721
Siegel, Paul Gerhard 459
Sivers, Jegor von 51
Smith, Charlotte K. 319
Spaulding, John A. 147
Stadelmann, Rudolf 32
Stahr, Adolf 52
Staiger, Emil 101
Stamm, Ralf 365
Stanger, Hermann 178
Stanguennoc, André 284, 285
Stanley, Robert 679
Steindecker, Werner 120
Steiner, Bernhard 264

Steinert, Walter 125
Stender-Petersen, A. 725
Stengel, E. 496
Stern, Adolf 45
Stern, Martin 597
Sternberg, A. von 46
Stickney-Bailey, Susan 286
Stokoe, F.W. 672
Stopp, Elisabeth 7, 115, 168
Strack, Friedrich 619
Stricker, Käthe 70
Strohschneider-Kohrs, Ingrid 191, 192
Süss, Wilhelm 188
Sulger-Gebing, Emil 694
Swales, Martin 320
Sydow, A. 53
Szafarz, Jolanta 217
Szondi, Peter 193

Taraba, Wolfgang F. 460
Tatar, Maria 321, 337
Tecchi, Bonaventura 102, 255, 696
Teich, Gabriel 263
Teichmann, Elisabeth 678
Thalmann, Marianne 8, 103, 104, 112, 118, 126, 131, 142, 148, 198, 199, 287, 288, 366, 423, 424
Ticknor, Anna 531
Todsen, Hermann 289
Todt, August Wilhelm 143
Trainer, James 33, 61, 89, 137, 256, 425, 476, 477, 608

Uechtritz, Maria 506
Ulshöfer, Robert 175

Vetterlund, Fredrik 727

Viëtor, Karl 461
Vitt-Maucher, Gisela 322
Vredeveld, Harry 338

Walzel, Oskar 478
Weibel, Oskar 462
Weigand, Karlheinz 323, 426, 427
Weiss, Hermann 497
Weissert, Otto 565
Wellek, René 557
Weller, Maximilian 47
Wells, Larry D. 290
Wendriner, Karl Georg 176
Wenger, Karl 452
Wernaer, Robert M. 105
Werner, Karl 689
Wesollek, Peter 257
Wetzel, Johannes Volkmar 598
Wheeler, Kathleen 62
Whiting, George W. 680
Whitinger, Raleigh 339
Wiedemann-Lambinus, Margarete 632
Wieneke, Ernst 486
Wiens, Abram G. 367
Wiese, Benno von 395
Willoughby, L.A. 63
Wohlrab, Anna 710
Wohnlich, Oskar 714
Wolf, Jacques 210
Wolff, Kurt 481
Wührl, Paul-Wolfgang 291
Wüstling, Fritz 428
Wunderlich, Werner 266

Zeising, Adolf 54
Zelak, Dominik 218
Zeydel, Edwin H. 23, 58, 64,

65, 71-73, 81, 106, 171, 180,
368, 464-466, 470, 473, 487,
501, 510, 527, 599, 668, 670
Ziegener, Thomas 24, 149
Zimmer, Heinrich W.B. 519
Zoeppritz, Rudolf 550
Zusman, V.G. 233

For Product Safety Concerns and Information please contact our EU representative GPSR@taylorandfrancis.com
Taylor & Francis Verlag GmbH, Kaufingerstraße 24, 80331 München, Germany

www.ingramcontent.com/pod-product-compliance
Lightning Source LLC
Chambersburg PA
CBHW052110300426
44116CB00010B/1611